REAL ESTATE BUYING/SELLING GUIDE FOR ONTARIO

REAL ESTATE BUYING/SELLING GUIDE FOR ONTARIO

Stanley M. Rose, B.A., LL.B.

International Self-Counsel Press Ltd.
Head and Editorial Office
Vancouver
Toronto   Seattle

Printed in Canada
First edition: May, 1973
Second edition: October, 1975
Third edition: July, 1977
Fourth edition: October, 1979
Fifth edition: November, 1981
Sixth edition: May, 1985
Seventh edition: August, 1987

Canadian Cataloguing in Publication Data

Rose, Stanley M., 1943-
  Real estate buying-selling guide for Ontario

  (Self-counsel series)
  ISBN 0-88908-364-9

  1. Vendors and purchasers — Ontario — Popular works. 2. House buying — Ontario. 3. House selling — Ontario. I. Title. II. Series.
KE0271.Z82R57 1987 346.71304′36 C87-091330-1

International Self-Counsel Press Ltd.
Head and Editorial Office
1481 Charlotte Road
North Vancouver, British Columbia V7J 1H1
Vancouver Toronto Seattle

CONTENTS

v

LIST OF SAMPLES

FOREWORD

For most people, the purchase of a home represents the largest single expenditure of their lifetime. Yet many people make offers to purchase homes without first getting all of the answers to their questions and, even more important, without knowing what questions to ask.

Similarly, selling the home can be equally important to allow one to move into a larger home or to provide for retirement.

No one wants to pay too much for a home or buy a home that will create more problems than it solves. No one wants to accept too low a price for their home or make an agreement that cannot be kept. Yet how do you avoid these things?

You should ask yourself these questions: What can a real estate agent do for me? How much should I pay or accept? What about the mortgage? Can I rent the basement or the upstairs rooms? How do I know that the house will be finished on time? What does my lawyer do for me and how much will I have to pay? When can I move in or out? The list goes on and on.

In this book you will not find definite answers to all of your questions. Nor will you learn how to buy or sell a house without retaining a lawyer. The purpose is to give you guidelines as to what you should think about when buying and selling your home and what areas to consider in order to avoid unfortunate surprises.

There are several areas of the law and several things your lawyer does that you should know about in order to discuss your transaction with him or her and better understand what he or she is trying to communicate to you.

Finally, through the use of sample forms, you can see what some of the documentation in a residential real estate transaction will look like and why it is necessary. In order to make this publication useful for everyone, the subject is discussed from a practical viewpoint and in a general frame of reference. Specific problems and technical complexities are best left to your lawyer.

The author wishes to acknowledge with thanks the assistance of Heather Rhynold, who prepared the manuscript, and Gerald Ross whose ideas and criticisms were extremely valuable.

1

WHAT SHOULD YOU PAY FOR A HOUSE?

a. SO, YOU WANT TO BUY A HOUSE

It is a sad fact that in many urban areas in Ontario today, many families simply cannot afford to own a fully detached home and, in fact, in some of these areas, it is extremely difficult for families to own any type of house including a condominium. Part of the reason for this fact is the high cost of developing land into building lots and the similarly high cost of maintaining "acceptable community planning" principles.

It is not the function of this book to lament the reasons why this unfortunate situation exists, but merely to point out that, while the idea of owning your own home is still firmly entrenched in our collective North American minds, a smaller and smaller number of people are capable of realizing this goal. This is especially true in or near metropolitan centres where it is impossible to find a vacant piece of dirt of reasonable size for under $35 000. If this piece of dirt is serviced with water, sewers, roads, street lighting and sidewalks, it may easily cost $60 000 or $70 000 or even more in today's urban market.

As a result of this economic necessity you may be forced to consider alternatives to buying a fully detached home. Such alternatives include renting (apartments, town-houses, semi-detached or detached houses) or buying less expensive accommodation (semi-detached, condominium or co-operative apartment or townhouse). All of these are a result of efforts to utilize available land more efficiently, thus decreasing the total cost of housing.

It is the goal of this book to provide current and practical information about various forms of home-ownership and the best procedure to achieve such ownership. It is hoped that such information will help you avoid pitfalls and save money when buying a home.

1

b. THE DOWN PAYMENT

One of the most difficult problems for the prospective home buyer in today's urban home market is saving enough money for the down payment. Today there are many demands placed on our disposable income. A prospective home buyer must be fortunate enough to have a large income or a large supply of money available for a down payment. Of necessity then there will be some sacrifices involved, and like anything else the less you are required to borrow, the better your position will be in making monthly payments.

The purchase price of a home is divided into two amounts — the down payment and the unpaid purchase price — which is usually financed with a mortgage. Therefore, a substantial down payment, as compared to a moderate down payment, will either decrease the amount of the carrying charges, or alternatively, allow you to buy a more expensive home. After reading the rest of this chapter, you should be able to determine your financial limitations regarding the down payment and the amount of carrying charges. From this it is easy to determine the price range of the home that you can afford.

c. HOW MUCH SHOULD YOU SPEND ON HOUSING?

It is generally accepted that a family should spend no more than one-third of its total gross income on "housing." This figure may vary from individual to individual, depending on other financial commitments but, in the vast majority of cases, this figure should not be exceeded. If it is exceeded, the family is, in all likelihood, in a precarious position where the slightest disruption or emergency could trigger a financial crisis. In arriving at the amount that you can afford to spend on housing, you should include the cost of the following items:

(a) Mortgage payments

(b) Property taxes

(c) Fire and liability insurance

(d) Heating, electricity, and water charges

(e) Maintenance — including interior and exterior re-painting and occasional repair of the roof and of electrical, plumbing, and heating systems (among others)

(f) Gardening

1. Mortgage payments

Generally the interest rate of the mortgage is set at the time the mortgage is arranged. If the agreement for the purchase of the home calls for a closing soon after the agreement has been signed, the interest rate under the mortgage is able to be determined at the time of mortgage approval. However, most banks and mortgage companies will not make a commitment to hold an interest rate at a specified level for an indefinite or a very long period of time and, therefore, if the agreement of purchase and sale calls for a delayed closing date, as is the case in many purchases of new homes, the interest rate under the mortgage will not be able to be determined until approximately 30 or 60 days before the actual closing date. The attitude from time to time of lending institutions in this regard is related to the stability or volatility of interest rates in the market place. For example, in the early 1980s, when interest rates were changing by large amounts on a very frequent (some-times weekly) basis, lenders would only commit to a speci-fied mortgage interest rate for 30 or 60 days, and in the last months of 1986 and the early months of 1987, when inter-est rates were quite stable (i.e., changing by very small amounts and staying at that level for long periods of time), borrowers were able to obtain commitments from mort-gage lenders to hold the interest rate at a specified amount or within a specified range of interest rates for up to six months and sometimes even longer. When interest rates are unstable, lenders will usually approve purchasers in the early stages of the transaction and then determine the interest rate to be charged under the mortgage some 30 or 60 days before the time the funds are actually advanced.

3

The importance of fixing the interest rate is that the amount of the monthly mortgage payment is dependent on the amount of interest being charged under the mortgage over the term of the mortgage. In conventional mortgages, the larger part of the mortgage payment is applied against the current accumulated interest, while the remaining part is applied against the principal sum borrowed (the "principal"). When mortgage payments cover only principal and interest they are referred to as "P. & I." payments.

2. Property taxes

Many mortgage lenders stipulate in their mortgage that they will pay the property taxes so they can ensure that the property taxes are paid. In such cases, and assuming one has a conventional mortgage with monthly payments, one-twelfth of the estimated yearly taxes is added to the total monthly payments. Such a mortgage is called a "P.I. and T." (principal, interest and taxes) mortgage.

The payments on such a mortgage will vary from year to year depending on the rise in property taxes. If the property taxes are not included in the mortgage, you would be wise to set aside a monthly amount which would cover the yearly property taxes when they are payable to the municipality. Many people who do not do this find themselves unable to suddenly raise the money at tax time and consequently are forced to either borrow the outstanding amount or pay the late payment penalty.

Most municipalities have instituted a procedure requiring you to pay property taxes in instalments (from two to eight payments, depending on the municipality) during the year. This benefits you by spreading out your payments and it benefits the municipality by providing it with a more even flow of revenue. Remember to allow for a yearly increase in property taxes of 5% to 8% or even more.

3. Fire and liability insurance

The standard home owner insurance policy not only insures against the risk of damage by fire to the dwelling, but also provides coverage against loss to the contents of

4

the house and, in addition, coverage against personal liability and property damage (i.e., when someone gets hurt on the property or someone's property becomes damaged as a result of the owner's negligence). The amount of the dwelling coverage should be sufficient to cover the replacement value of the building that is to be insured — as opposed to the purchase price, which would also include the land and the foundation of the house and which may have no relationship at all to the cost of repairing damage to the house. The land and the foundation of the house cannot be destroyed and, therefore, the insurance coverage does not have to consider these costs.

The amount of insurance carried under some policies automatically increases every year to take into account the rising replacement cost due to inflation. Even if your insurance policy does this automatically, you should still be sure to review your insurance coverage (and we suggest that this be done annually) to make sure that your coverage keeps up with inflation. Otherwise, in the event of a loss, you will find that the insurance proceeds do not cover the cost of repairing or replacing the damage.

Formerly, insurance policies were written for a three-year period, with the premium payable in advance, but it is now more common for insurance policies to be written for one year only. When budgeting the cost of insurance, you should remember that not only are insurance rates subject to change, but also, as replacement values escalate, an increase in insurance coverage will result in a corresponding increase in the premium. Please note that coverage for stamps, jewellery and other such items — as well as earthquake and flood coverage — is, in most instances, not included in the policy unless specifically requested and unless an additional premium is paid.

4. Utility charges

In calculating the approximate amount of utility charges, you should remember to average these out over the entire year, as both heating and electricity (and, in some cases, water charges, where they are metered) will vary according to the season. For estimating purposes, be sure to obtain this information from the vendor before submitting an offer. You may be wise to request receipts, as many property owners' estimates of their charges are only wild guesses. Remember, too, that utility rates are subject to increases. If in doubt, ask your friends or relatives who are home owners, what they pay.

5. Maintenance
Although it is impossible to determine the exact amount required for maintenance and repairs, it is wise to allocate a monthly figure in excess of the bare maintenance costs. Remember, it is impossible to anticipate all expenses, and some amount should be allowed for "major replacement" expenditures.

In arriving at a realistic amount, you should consider how often the interior and exterior will need repainting or refinishing, how often floor coverings such as linoleum or carpet will need replacing, how often plumbing or electrical wiring will need to be repaired, how often the furnace or hot water tank will need an overhaul, etc.

6. Gardening
In estimating gardening expenses, you should consider the cost of maintaining the garden as well as the initial cost of garden equipment such as lawn mowers, edgers, rakes, shears, shovels, ladders, and hoses.

7. Don't forget those initial expenses
We have just looked at the continuing expenses of owning a house once it has been acquired. However, there are several initial expenses that should also be considered:

(a) Moving costs

(b) The need for appliances such as a refrigerator, stove, dishwasher, washer, and dryer

(c) Redecorating costs, including carpets and draperies

(d) Legal fees, disbursements and land transfer tax

(e) Other adjustments

The above are self-explanatory with the exception of (e). "Other adjustments" would include additional items that the purchaser is required to pay the vendor (the seller).

These are usually reimbursements of expenses that the vendor has prepaid on behalf of the purchaser — such as fuel oil in the tank, fire insurance (if the purchaser is assuming the vendor's policy), prepaid taxes, and water rates.

Adjustments of these items are covered between the vendor and the purchaser in a document known as the "Statement of Adjustments." This statement adjusts figures and amounts owed by both parties as of the adjustment date, and it is usually prepared by the vendor's lawyer. (This document will be discussed in further detail later.) As these items are additional expenses that are not included in the down payment, you, as the purchaser, should be very careful before committing your entire savings to such a down payment. A few weeks before closing, ask your lawyer the exact amount of money required on the closing date in order to avoid a surprise at the last moment.

Let's use an example to illustrate how a prospective purchaser can determine an affordable price range for a home.

Peter and Paula Purchaser have saved $20 000 and now wish to purchase a house. Peter and Paula both work full time and earn approximately $36 000 in combined gross income per year. Peter expects that he will be making that by himself in approximately two years when they expect Paula to stop working to have a family. They feel that they will have to purchase appliances for about $1 800 and have estimated that their other initial expenses will be about $1 200 — total outlay of $3 000. This will leave them with a down payment of $20 000 minus $3 000, or $17 000.

Since 30% of their gross income is $10 800 per year or $900 per month, Peter and Paula should, therefore, be able to afford to spend approximately $900 per month on housing without overextending themselves. A conventional mortgage which is amortized (calculated according to the length of time that it takes to repay the mortgage based on fixed payments and a fixed interest rate) over 25 years at 12% interest requires monthly payments of just over $100 for every $10 000 borrowed. However, if the interest on the mortgage was 10% per annum, over $11 000 could be obtained with the same monthly payment.

Peter and Paula have calculated that, for a house in the $80 000 to $100 000 bracket, their continuing expenses would be as follows:

Property taxes	$1 200 per year
Fire and liability insurance	150 per year
Water	120 per year
Electricity	500 per year
Maintenance	250 per year
Gardening	180 per year
Total (approximate only)	**$2 400 per year** or **$200 per month**

Therefore, Peter and Paula Purchaser should not spend more on a house than $70 000 plus $17 000, i.e., $87 000 — if the interest rate on their mortgage is 12%, or $94 000 ($77 000 plus $17 000) if their mortgage is 10%.

This example and the generally accepted rules apply to the average family situation. It goes without saying that if a person is already heavily indebted, these ratios will not work. Likewise, they will not work without a sacrifice of some sort if an extraordinary amount of income is usually spent on hobbies or other items.

Another pitfall to be wary of is that most prospective home buyers fall in love with, and want to buy, the home that is just a little bit above their budget. This overreaching will, in many cases, not be discouraged by the real estate agent whose commission is based on the sales price.

Some people will unwisely argue that such overreaching is justified, as inflation will undoubtedly mean salary increases while the largest cost of owning a house, namely the mortgage payment, will remain constant. Therefore, they rationalize that, as time goes by, they will be better able to afford the house. Unfortunately, it is not always possible to foresee financial setbacks, which in the case of the overextended purchaser, could result in a severe crunch and possibly in financial disaster.

2

SOME THINGS YOU SHOULD KNOW ABOUT CONTRACTS

a. THE OFFER TO PURCHASE BECOMES THE AGREEMENT OF PURCHASE AND SALE

An agreement to buy or sell land and buildings is a contract and, like any contract, must meet certain requirements. The "contract" relating to the sale of land is usually an agreement of purchase and sale; the only differences between this contract and any other contract are that the agreement of purchase and sale deals with land and the amount of money at stake is very large, and the contract, to be enforceable, must be in writing.

Therefore, you should know something about contracts before buying or selling a home. We can't, of course, discuss all of the laws relating to contracts, nor can we fully discuss the areas that are included in this book (every rule has it exceptions). What we are trying to point out in this chapter is some of the basic matters relating to a contract in order to help you understand what you are doing when you sign or alter the agreement of purchase and sale. Don't try to be a lawyer, but you should understand what you are getting into.

The offer to purchase is *probably the most important legal document you will ever sign.* For this reason, it should *not* be considered as the beginning of the transaction, but rather should be considered as the climax of all of your planning and forethought. Once signed, the offer to purchase becomes an agreement of purchase and sale.

This document provides the foundation for almost the whole transaction. It serves to define, determine and limit both the obligations and rights of both parties until the transaction is completed and in some instances, even afterwards.

An offer to purchase must be in writing to be enforceable. It need not be a formal contract (such as the standard printed forms); a memorandum or letter will suffice so long as it identifies the parties to the contract, sets forth the terms agreed upon and is signed by the person liable.

A word of warning here. Because of the importance of this document, be sure to obtain competent advice on the drafting of the terms. A do-it-yourself offer can sometimes be more dangerous than useful.

b. REQUIREMENTS OF A CONTRACT

The agreement of purchase and sale must meet the basic requirements of all contracts, which are as follows:

(a) All of the parties to the contract must be under no *legal disability*, i.e., such as being an infant, insane or drunk.

(b) Each party under the contract must receive a benefit, commonly called consideration; or, alternatively, it must be placed under seal (red stickers placed beside your name).

(c) Each party to the contract must intend to create a legal relationship between himself or herself and the other parties to the contract. In other words, the parties must intend to be bound to the obligations in the contract.

(d) The contract, after all of its terms have been negotiated, must be agreed upon by all of the parties to the contract.

(e) The subject matter of the contract must not be something that is prohibited by law, e.g., gambling house. The courts will not enforce a contract where the object of the contract is either illegal or immoral.

1. Legal disability

The law recognizes that certain classes of people are unable to enter into a contractual relationship and,

10

accordingly, will not enforce a contract against such a person. Such people include infants (people who are under the legal age requirement), people with mental disorders, people under the influence of liquor and perhaps drugs, and corporations under certain circumstances.

In Ontario, an infant is a person who is under the age of 18 years and an infant is unable to be bound by a contract unless the contract is for necessaries or is beneficial to the infant. Thus, in Ontario an infant is not able to deal with land, because ownership of land is not considered necessary or beneficial.

It may be difficult to determine whether a person is mentally disordered to the extent that the courts will not enforce a contract against that person but, once this determination is made, such a person will not be held to be bound by a contract.

A person who is under the influence of liquor and perhaps drugs (it is not known whether the law will equally apply to persons who are under the influence of drugs), will not be held to be obligated to the other party if it can be shown that the person was incapable of understanding what he or she was doing and that the other party was aware of this condition. However, if the party who was not incapable has assigned his or her rights under the contract to a third party or if a third party is involved in the contract and some rights accrue to this third party, the person who was incapable by reason of drink may be held liable under the contract.

A corporation may be unable to enter into a contract unless all of the matters pertaining to the contract are within its powers. A corporation is created by statute and is governed by statute, a charter, and the internal constitution of the corporation consisting of its by-laws and resolutions. Thus, if a corporation attempts to do something that is not permitted to be done within this constitution, it may be held by a court of law that the corporation is not liable under this contract.

2. Consideration or seal

You may be asked to sign a contract "under seal." A seal need not be an instrument that creates an impression on the document or a round red wafer with adhesive back. A seal may be anything that indicates that the party who has applied the seal to the document has given a great deal of thought to the contents of that document.

If a contract is under seal, it may be that it is not necessary for the person who has signed that contract to receive any benefit at all from the contract. However, if a contract is not under seal, it is necessary to show that the person against whom the contract is sought to be enforced received a benefit under the contract.

The sufficiency of the benefit is not the paramount factor and, in fact, is not relevant to the determination of whether the document is a contract. It only matters that the person sought to be held liable received a benefit. However, it must be remembered that the benefit that a person receives must be a benefit that the party is not already entitled to receive. For example, if Barb Borrower promises to give Larry Lender his book back upon payment of $5, Larry will not be held liable under the contract because he was already entitled to his own book.

In a real estate transaction, there is usually no problem relating to consideration or the requirement of a seal because the vendor receives, by way of consideration, the purchaser's promise to pay and the purchaser receives, by way of consideration, the vendor's promise to convey the property.

3. Intention to be bound by the contract

The parties to a contract must form the intention that they will be bound by the contract and, accordingly, if they fail to discharge their obligations under the contract, they will be subject to legal consequences. Again, in a real estate transaction, because of the nature and size of the obligations involved, it is difficult to conceive of anyone entering into such a contract without having the necessary intention to be bound by the obligations under the contract.

12

4. Mutual agreement

The contract and all of its terms must be agreed upon by all of the parties to the contract. This is often considered to be the doctrine of "mutual agreement" or the doctrine of "offer and acceptance." This doctrine recognizes that in the bargaining process, one party offers and the other party may agree or counter-offer. The importance of this aspect of the law of contract is that once the negotiation has been completed, all of the parties to the contract must agree that all of the terms in the contract form a part of the contract and that there are no other terms involved. Thus, negotiations will usually begin with an offer and, in real estate transactions, this offer will usually be in writing.

An offer, once made, will be an outstanding obligation on behalf of the person who made the offer until one of the following things happens.

(a) The offer, by its terms, expires. An example of this type of situation is where Bob Buyer offers to buy Sue Seller's home and states to Sue that she must accept the offer, if at all, within 48 hours. At the end of the 48 hours, the offer, by its own terms, lapses.

(b) The death of either the person making the offer or the person to whom the offer was made.

(c) The rejection of the offer by the person to whom it was made.

(d) The making of a counter-offer by the person to whom the original offer was made. This is, in effect, a refusal of the original offer and the making of a new offer to the original offeror. In this regard, it is important to keep in mind that there is a difference between a counter-offer and a request for information. For example, Eddie Eager may say to Harry Hesitant, "I will sell you my house for $1 000." If Harry replies, "I will give you $900 for your house," he has made a counter-offer. However, if Harry replies, "Will you accept $900 for your house?" it may be held that he was not making a counter-offer, but was merely asking a question.

(e) The party who makes the offer may revoke the offer unless the offer is under seal for a certain specified period of time or unless the party who has made the offer has received some consideration for allowing the offer to remain outstanding for a specified period of time. The latter matter is often considered to be an option in that a person is given a certain amount of money for making an offer and allowing the offer to remain open for acceptance for a specific period of time by another party. It is important to remember that if an offer is to be revoked, it must be revoked before it is accepted because once it is accepted, the offer and acceptance together form a contract. In addition the revocation of an offer must be brought to the attention of the person to whom the offer was made before it takes effect.

An offer must be complete in order to form the basis of a contract. The courts will hesitate to complete a contract for two parties if the contract of the parties is not sufficiently certain. It is for this reason that a listing or advertisement is not considered an "offer to sell" but merely an "invitation to negotiate" — there are many matters other than price to be agreed upon.

An acceptance of an offer must be communicated to the person who has made the offer and must be unconditional. If an offer states the exact manner in which it is to be accepted, the acceptance must be in this manner. For example, an offer that contains a provision that acceptance must be made by carrier pigeon only, will not be accepted if the acceptance is communicated by telegram.

If no manner of acceptance is specified, the acceptance of an offer may be by express acceptance communicated to the person who has made the offer or by implication, perhaps by the performance of an act indicating acceptance. For example, if Bob Buyer says to Sue Seller that he will buy Sue's house for $25 000 cash payable on December 12, next, and if Sue subsequently lets Bob move into the house, Sue by her actions, may be deemed to have accepted Bob's offer.

However, an offer may not be accepted by silence, but rather, requires the positive act of the person accepting the offer. An acceptance *must* be unconditional to act as an acceptance forming a contract. If the acceptance deviates from the offer as made, the deviation may be deemed to be a rejection of the offer and the making of a counter-offer, which then requires the acceptance of the original offeror.

For example, if you offer to buy George Greedy's house for $25 000, with $5 000 down payment, $20 000 mortgage for 25 years at 10% interest with equal monthly payments, and if he replies, "Offer accepted at 10-1/2%," he has rejected your offer and has made a counter-offer that you may accept or reject.

c. BREACH OF CONTRACT

A contract should not only be sufficient in content but should specify the importance of the particular provision by stating whether it is a covenant, warranty, representation or condition. This is important because the law recognizes that there are different remedies for different forms of breach of the contract. In other words, if you are in breach of an obligation imposed by a contract, the injured party will have different remedies depending on the particular breach.

The actual remedy that is able to be recovered by the injured party depends in part upon the nature of the obligation that is breached. A breach of a *condition* in a contract allows the injured party to consider the contract to be at an end because a condition is considered to be of paramount importance to the person in whose favor the condition operates.

On the other hand, in many situations, a breach of a condition may permit the injured party to sue for completion of the contract and *also* for damages. Or, if the breach is a breach of warranty, the injured party merely has a right to damages and is not able to consider the contract to be at an end. *This area of the law is extremely technical*

15

and complicated and a complete discussion of this area of the law is beyond the scope of this book. However, it has been raised at this point in order to emphasize three facts.

(a) If a matter is of sufficient importance to a party to the contract, it should be set forth in the contract in such a way that any breach of the matter will allow the injured party to consider the contract to be at an end if it is so desired.

(b) If a breach of a term of a contract occurs, the contract is not necessarily at an end, but rather, the injured party should immediately seek legal advice in order to protect his or her interests.

(c) If you seek legal advice *before* signing the offer, your lawyer will be able to make the contract say what *you* want it to say.

d. THE USE OF STANDARD FORMS

Most agreements of purchase and sale entered into today are prepared on a standard form that is available from any of the suppliers of legal forms. Many people tend to think that a standard printed form cannot be changed. This is not so. The printed form is merely a guide for the convenience of the user, and can be changed, amended, added to or deleted from. (Remember to initial the changes.) The important fact is that the contract should include all the matters that are agreed upon by all the parties.

Samples #1 and #2 in chapter 3 are examples of offers for the purchase of an older home and the purchase of a new home respectively. Each started as an offer to purchase, was negotiated and finally agreed to by all parties. At this point, they both became agreements of purchase and sale.

The sample offers are not intended to be complete, nor are they intended for use in all such types of transactions. They are merely examples of what may be considered to be important to a particular vendor and purchaser. When two or more individuals negotiate a contract concerning a particular piece of property, there can be no hard and fast rules. Rather the product will be a result of negotiation and precise, complete *legal* drafting.

In other words, there is nothing that *must* be included in an agreement of purchase and sale, other than the basic requisites of a contract already discussed. Remember, you cannot be forced to sign a document, standard form or otherwise. Make sure that it contains everything you want and that you understand and agree to everything in it. If you don't like it, don't sign it!

(See, also, Interim Agreement forms available from Self-Counsel Press.)

3

HOW TO ACTUALLY SELECT
AND BUY A HOME

a. BE PREPARED TO SPEND A LOT OF ENERGY

Once you have determined the price range, you can actually start looking for a home. This can be hard work and should not be taken lightly. How many homes should you view before making a decision? The industry average seems to be eight. This is far too low a number. Three times that number should be the minimum number, for this would serve to increase your knowledge and perception about the housing market immeasurably. If you think about it, many ideas you have about the kind of home you want come from the direct viewing of other homes. So it stands to reason, the more you get to look at the better your chance of getting one to suit you.

A home is probably the biggest investment of most peoples' lives, and any errors involved in the purchase can be costly. First, decide what you require in housing and what you can realistically expect to obtain in your price range. Second, decide the general area in which the house should be located. Third, attempt to obtain some feel for what is available in the general area. Become familiar with price structure. There are a number of ways of doing this, such as looking through newspaper advertisements and publications offering homes for sale or, for instance, attending open houses. This is probably one of the best ways (although time-consuming) of being able to obtain the experience to enable you to judge and select a good buy rather than a poor one without relying entirely on an agent's or anyone's advice.

The chart on pages 19 and 20 lists many of the factors you should consider.

CHECK LIST FOR THE HOUSE BUYER

SITE DATA: Lot Size _____ x _____

EXPROERTY	SERVICES		ROAD TYPE		LANDSCAPING		SIZE OF LOT FOR AREA	
	Water		Paved		Good		Large	
	Gas		Gravel		Fair		Average	
	Sanitary Sewer		Curbs		Poor		Small	
	Septic Tank		Sidewalks					
	Storm Sewers							

EXBUILDING	TYPE		EXTERIOR		ROOF		PARKING - Capacity		DRIVEWAY	
	Detached		Brick		Asphalt/Duroid		Garage		Private	
	Semi-Detached		Stone		Cedar		Carport		Mutual	
	No. of Stories		Siding		Slate		None		Lane	
	Split		Stucco		Tar & Gravel					

INTERIOR	FLOOR PLAN		INTERIOR WALLS		BASEMENT		HEATING SYSTEM		FUEL		MAINTENANCE	
	Good		Plaster		Full		Hot Water		Coal		Excellent	
	Fair		Dry Wall		Partial		Gravity Air		Oil		Good	
	Poor		Paneling		None - Slab		Forced Air		Gas		Fair	
	Main Floor				None - Crawl		Electric		Conversion		Poor	
	Area sq. ft.											

19

FIREPLACE		INSULATION		WIRING	Amp. 60	100	HOT WATER		PLUMBING		FLOORS	
Open		Walls		New			Electric		Galvanized		Hardwood	
Electric		Ceiling		Old			Gas		Copper		Tile	
Gas		Roof		Adequate			Oil		Plastic		Carpet	
None							Capacity					

Number and Type of Rooms

	L/R	D/R	Kit.	B/R	BATH	WASH	FAM.	OTHER
Basement								
1st Floor								
2nd Floor								
Other								

KITCHEN		BATHROOM		LIVING ROOM		BEDROOMS		CLOSETS	
Excellent		New		Excellent		Large		Ample	
Good		Average		Good		Medium		Adequate	
Fair		Fair		Fair		Small		Fair	
Poor		Outdated		Poor				Inadequate	

b. THE REAL ESTATE SALESPERSON OR AGENT

By far the majority of homes are purchased through a real estate agent. Contact with an agent is most often made through an advertisement in the paper or by going to an agent's office directly and inquiring about a house. As is the same in any profession, the ability of real estate agents varies from individual to individual. The good, knowledgeable, and helpful real estate agent can be a tremendous asset both to a vendor and a purchaser. Therefore, if it is at all possible, attempt to get the best agent available either through a recommendation or by meeting a few and then selecting the one that suits your needs best.

When looking for an agent, try to select one who deals exclusively with houses in the area in which you are interested in settling. Some agents deal only with commercial or industrial real estate and some restrict their activities to limited geographical areas. This is especially so in the larger urban centres.

An agent will help you locate the house that is most suitable for you and negotiate with the vendor over price, terms, etc. An agent also usually writes the offer to purchase, or agreement of purchase and sale, and, therefore, should have a basic knowledge of real estate law. But always remember that a real estate agent is an adviser — he or she will not have to live in the house. Too often, potential purchasers are unwilling to reject the agent's advice.

Just because a particular house is listed with a certain real estate company does not necessarily mean that a prospective buyer has to contact that particular company. The purchaser can choose to contact any agent he or she wishes. Most agents co-operate with one another to the extent that an agent from A company who has a purchaser can approach the agent from B company who has the listing so that arrangements can be made to show the property to the prospective purchaser and, if the purchaser is interested enough, to present an offer to the vendor.

The real estate agents will, in this instance, split the commission if there is a sale. In many cases this is a more comfortable situation for both the purchaser and the vendor, as both parties will have an agent representing their interests, although legally both are agents of the vendor who customarily pays the commission. Since the agent who has the listing is paid on commission and by the vendor, that agent will try to secure the highest price possible while keeping in mind that it is better to sell a house at a lower price than not to sell it at all.

Most agents are also members of a multiple listing service which is a co-operative service between real estate agents serving the function of disseminating listing information to its members. This not only gives the listing a larger exposure, but also provides prospective purchasers with more selection. Such listings are given on listing sheets that usually contain a picture of each house and its specifications, such as the number of bathrooms, number of bedrooms, number of fireplaces, and square footage of the house. These enable prospective purchasers to narrow down their choices in the comfort of the real estate agent's office rather than having to invest the time and effort to actually inspect each house.

Before you even approach an agent, you should have some idea of what you want. Then the agent can immediately select the homes which meet these criteria rather than using the time-consuming method of trial and error which wastes time for everyone concerned. When you find "the one," try to make several inspections of the house prior to making an offer, so you can see the house both in the daytime and at night.

Occasionally you may run across a house that is being sold privately. At first you will be delighted at the thought of the vendor's not having to pay all that commission and, therefore, being able to offer you a lower price. However, this is not always true, as a vendor who does not have the property listed may intend to save that money, rather than passing it on to the purchaser. In addition, watch out for vendors who are merely "fishing" and have no real intention of selling. You can very quickly determine the motive of the vendor by comparing the asking price with other comparable homes in the area and by closely questioning the vendor as to the reasons for selling. A high asking price coupled with vague answers on the reason for selling mean that you should make a quick exit *even if you really like the house.* This house is probably not for sale.

In genuine "direct" sales, both the vendor and the purchaser should have some knowledge of real estate law as they may be writing the agreement themselves. If they do not have such knowledge, they should seek professional help either from a lawyer, notary, or a friend knowledgeable in real estate.

If an agreement of purchase and sale is signed, the vendor will, in all likelihood, want more than a token deposit, and consideration should be given as to who is to hold such a deposit and whether it is to be held in trust.

It is definitely *not* recommended that such a deposit be paid directly to the vendor. Instead, the deposit should be held in trust by the lawyer who should also be handling all of the money involved in the transaction.

c. BUYING A NEW HOME

1. General

When buying any type of home, whether it is new or old, it should be clearly understood by the purchaser that owning a home is time-consuming as well as expensive. There are always things that need to be done around the house if the house and property are to be kept in good repair. If it is not redecorating, it is fixing the plumbing, repairing the leak in the roof, winterizing the home, attending to the garden, and so on.

This is so even with a new house. As a matter of fact, some new houses may be even more time-consuming, as they usually require the basement and landscaping to be completed. This time factor is often overlooked by people purchasing a home, with the consequence that many people who do not have enough time to spend on their homes find the experience very frustrating. Such people

23

may be better served by owning a townhouse where many of the time-consuming chores are done for them.

Keeping down the cost of housing is difficult. Mass production in the building of houses can save the builder money, and some of these savings can be passed on to the purchaser. Mass production in home building, however, also means that a builder is limited to a smaller selection of styles. This, unfortunately, also means less selection for the purchaser.

By pre-selling homes either from model homes or from plans and specifications, a builder can save additional money since, if the home is already sold, the transaction can be completed immediately upon completion of the home; thus the builder will not be required to pay the carrying charges for the period from the time of completion to the time it is sold. On any larger project this could be a considerable saving. It also allows the purchaser more choice in colors of carpets, bathroom fixtures, etc. Further reductions by the builder can be obtained since more favorable contracts can be negotiated with suppliers and subtrades when negotiating with volume.

When purchasing a home from inspection of plans and specifications, you encounter the difficulty of having to form a visual concept of what the completed house will look like after its construction. Thus, you must visualize the completed product and then determine what deviations or additions to construction are required for your purposes. This is extremely difficult and even the artist's conceptions can be of little assistance.

In addition, when purchasing a home from the inspection of plans and specifications, it is even more difficult to determine the *quality* of the items that will be included in the construction, such as the broadloom, wallpaper, floor covering, tiles, etc. Therefore, you should be very careful when purchasing a home by this method and we recommend retaining an independent person knowledgeable in the construction of houses to advise you. If you aren't able to locate someone directly, you may consider joining a home owner's association. In the past few years, many private firms have entered the housing scene to offer consulting and inspection services.

Although your alternatives are somewhat limited when purchasing a mass-produced home, some choices are still available. Once you have decided on the model, you are able to choose, from a limited number, the color of the exterior and/or the interior and the color of the bathroom fixtures, carpets, etc. Any further changes or additional items may not be available and even if they are, they will be "extras" for which the cost will be added on to the purchase price.

Reference to all color choices made and extras required should be included either in the agreement itself or in a schedule attached to the agreement. The same applies where the builder agrees to any out-of-the-ordinary deviations — for example, if certain appliances that you want are not available from the builder and have to be installed as extras. The builder may, however, be prepared to give you an "appliance credit" on the purchase price and then not install any appliances whatsoever. Then you will be able to obtain your own appliances and have them installed. There are, of course, an unlimited number of such deviations and they should be included in the agreement to protect both parties.

A sample agreement of purchase and sale reproduced as Sample #1 contains many clauses that may be contained in a builder's standard contract form. It is not suggested that this form is unduly harsh on a purchaser, but you will certainly notice that much of the contract involves obligations on the purchaser.

The agreement of purchase and sale that is provided by the builder for signature by the purchaser has been prepared by the builder's lawyer, and, of course, is usually weighted in the builder's favor. However, many builders realize that their success is directly related to their reputation and, accordingly, will instruct their lawyer to prepare an agreement of purchase and sale that protects them to a substantial degree but does not discourage a prospective purchaser.

SAMPLE #1
AGREEMENT OF PURCHASE AND SALE
(New Home)

WE, VICTOR VENDOR and VERNA VENDOR, (as Purchasers) hereby agree to and with NEW HOUSE BUILDERS LIMITED, (as Vendor) to purchase all and singular, the premises situated on the east side of Some Street, in the Borough of Scarborough, in the Municipality of Metropolitan Toronto, and known as House No. 629571 Some Street, having a frontage of about 60 feet more or less by a depth of about 110 feet more or less, being Lot Number 10625, according to Plan Number M-66666, filed in the Office of Land Titles at Toronto, at the price of FIFTY-ONE THOUSAND .($51,000.00) DOLLARS, as follows:

1.   THREE THOUSAND ($3,000.00) DOLLARS certified cheque made payable to the Vendor on this date as a deposit and the Purchaser covenants, promises and agrees to pay on closing the sum of ELEVEN THOUSAND ($11,000.00) DOLLARS, subject to the usual adjustments, and to assume a first mortgage of about THIRTY-SEVEN THOUSAND ($37,000.00) DOLLARS, bearing interest at the rate of 8 3/4% per annum, calculated half-yearly, not in advance, having an original term of 25 years and being repayable in monthly instalments of $320.00, which includes both principal and interest, and being amortized on a 25-year plan.

2.   The Vendor agrees to complete construction of the dwelling on the real property in accordance with the plans and specifications filed with the first mortgagee and in accordance with the provisions of Schedule "A" attached hereto. Vendor shall have the right to substitute other material for that provided for in these plans and specifications, subject to the approval by the first mortgagee.

3.   Purchaser covenants and agrees as follows:

      a) If first mortgagee does not approve of Purchaser, then, at the option of the Vendor, the within Agreement shall be null and void and the deposit shall be returned to the Purchaser without interest or deduction;

      b) That the Purchaser will, forthwith upon demand, execute and deliver all documents and assurances required by the first mortgagee pertaining to the first mortgage and its assumption by the Purchaser, including without limitation, all applications, Assumption Agreements, covenants by Purchaser and his or her spouse, proofs of income, proofs of occupancy, certifications of completion, declarations as to executions, power of attorney to endorse mortgage advance cheques, endorsements of mortgage advance cheques, irrevocable directions to pay unadvanced mortgage monies to Vendor and authorities to register releases of site plan and subdivision agreements;

      c) That the Purchaser will not cause this Agreement or any Caution or other document relating to this Agreement or claiming any interest in the real property to be registered against the title to the real property;

      d) Both before and after closing, that the Purchaser will not mortgage, sell, rent, deal with or encumber the real property in any way until such time as the Vendor has received the full amount of the first mortgage;

e) That the Vendor will retain a Vendor's Lien against the real property for any unadvanced portion of the first mortgage until the first mortgage has been fully advanced;

f) That in the event that completion of the dwelling on the real property is delayed for any reason whatsoever, that Vendor shall be permitted an extension of time for closing of up to 60 days and the time of closing shall be extended accordingly. If at the end of such extended period, the Vendor shall have been unable to complete the building on the real property, this Agreement shall be terminated, at the option of the Purchaser, and the deposit shall be returned to the Purchaser without interest or deduction whatsoever and the Vendor shall not be liable to the Purchaser for any damages whatsoever. It is understood and agreed that the dwelling on the real property shall be conclusively deemed to have been completed if all interior work, save for minor items of construction, shall be completed;

g) That Vendor shall have the right in the nature of an easement at any time or times within three years after closing for itself and persons authorized by it to enter upon the real property at all reasonable hours for inspection, repair and modification to the same and the Deed or Transfer in favour of the Purchaser may be subject to such right;

h) That there shall be no holdback under the Construction Lien Act or for any reason whatsoever and that the full balance of the purchase price will be paid to the Vendor on closing;

i) That the covenants of the Purchaser hereinbefore contained shall not merge with the delivery and registration of the Transfer to the Purchaser.

4.   The Vendor agrees to provide on closing a guarantee guaranteeing the plumbing and heating systems and the electrical wiring in the dwelling constructed on the real property for a period of one year following closing.

5.   Provided that the title is good and free from all encumbrances except as aforesaid and except as to any registered restrictions or covenants that run with the land provided the same have been complied with and except that the title may be subject to reasonable easements, rights-of-way, licenses, subdivision agreements as determined by the Vendor, for telephone, hydro and municipal services. The title is to be examined by the Purchaser at his own expense and he is not to call for the production of any title deeds or abstracts of title, proof or evidence of title, or to have furnished any copies thereof other than those in the Vendor's possession or under its control. The Purchaser is to be allowed 30 days from the date of acceptance hereof to examine the title at his own expense and if within that time he shall furnish the Vendor in writing with any valid objections to the title which the Vendor shall be unwilling or unable to remove and which the Purchaser will not waive, this agreement shall be null and void and the deposit money shall be returned without interest and the Vendor shall not be liable for any costs or damages whatsoever. Save as to any valid objections so made within such time, the Purchaser shall be conclusively deemed to have accepted the title of the Vendor to the real property. This transaction to be completed on or before the 30th day of June, 198-, subject to the Vendor's right to extend such closing, as

-3-

aforesaid. Unearned fire insurance premiums, taxes, local improvements, mortgage interest, water and assessment rates and fuel to be apportioned as of the date of closing.

6.   It is understood and agreed that there is no representation, warranty, collateral agreement or condition affecting this Agreement or supported hereby other than as expressed herein in writing. The dwelling on the real property shall be and remain at the risk of the Vendor until closing. In the event of damage to the dwelling on the real property, Vendor may either repair the damage and finish the dwelling on the real property and complete the sale or may cancel the within Agreement and have all monies theretofore paid returned to Purchaser without interest. Each party is to pay the costs of the preparation, registration and tax on his own documents and time shall in all respects be of the essence of this Agreement.

7.   The within Agreement shall enure to the benefit of Vendor, its successors and assigns and be binding upon the Purchaser, his heirs, executors, administrators and assigns.

8.   This Agreement shall be read with all changes of gender and number required by the context.

9.   This Offer shall be irrevocable by Purchaser and open for acceptance by Vendor until midnight of the 11th day of May, 198-, after which time if not accepted, the within Offer shall be null and void and the deposit shall be returned to Purchaser without interest, deduction or abatement whatsoever.

10.   Tender of any documents or monies deliverable or payable hereunder may be made by the Vendor or the Purchaser on the solicitor for the other party.

DATED this 5th day of May, 198—

SIGNED, SEALED & DELIVERED   )
  - in the presence of -   )
)   (signed) *Victor Vendor*
(signed)   )
      R.F. Agent   )   (signed) *Verna Vendor*
)
)
)

Vendor hereby accepts the above Offer and its terms and covenants, promises and agrees to and with the Purchaser to duly carry out the same on the terms and conditions above mentioned, this 10th day of May, 198—

NEW HOUSE BUILDERS LIMITED

per: (signed) *N.H. Builder*

Schedule "A" attached to and forming
part of the Offer to Purchase between
VICTOR and VERNA VENDOR and NEW HOUSE
BUILDERS LIMITED, regarding Lot 10625,
Plan M-66666, Office of Land Titles at
Toronto

1.   The purchase price of the real property, as hereinbefore
set forth, shall include the following work and materials which shall be
supplied and installed by Vendor:

      a) Solid masonry construction;
      b) Concrete block basement;
      c) 200 amp. electrical service;
      d) Natural gas forced hot air furnace;
      e) Electric light fixtures;
      f) Ceramic wall tile to ceiling in bathtub
         enclosures and coloured plumbing fixtures
         in all bathrooms;
      g) Kitchen cabinets, as per model;
      h) Double stainless steel sink in kitchen;
      i) Exhaust fan and hood in kitchen;
      j) Two exterior water taps;
      k) Private attached single garage and asphalt
         paved driveway;
      l) Precast concrete slab patio in rear;
      m) Carpeting on stairs from ground floor to
         second floor;
      o) Vinyl asbestos tile on floors of bathrooms,
         kitchen and front hall;
      p) Parquet floors in all bedrooms, living room,
         dining room, den and hallways.

2.   Purchaser shall not have a choice as to colour for any
work or materials completed prior to acceptance of the within Agreement
of Purchase and Sale by Vendor and shall have choice of colour from Vendor's
samples with respect to uncompleted work and materials which said choice
must be exercised by the Purchaser in writing within 10 days after
acceptance by Vendor of the within Agreement of Purchase and Sale, failing
which, Vendor shall have the absolute right to make colour selections
on Purchaser's behalf.

(signed) *Victor Vendor*

(signed) *Verna Vendor*

NEW HOUSE BUILDERS LIMITED

per: (signed) *N.H. Builder*

Another area in which you may have a limited choice is in the mortgage financing. Many builders arrange their construction financing in such a way that, on completion of the house, such financing becomes a conventional mortgage to be assumed by the purchaser. This could be a disadvantage to you if the mortgage financing does not fit your requirements.

On the other hand, it could be an advantage, as you would be spared the ordeal of searching for financing of your own and paying the costs incurred in connection with obtaining such financing. These costs could include fees for an appraisal, a survey and the legal documentation, to mention some of the most common. If the financing does not suit your needs, the builder may not be prepared to sell the house since the mortgage company may not be prepared to accept payment of the money prematurely, or, even if it would, the builder may not be prepared to absorb the prepayment penalty that the mortgage company assesses in these cases.

2. Completion and moving dates

One of the main concerns that you will encounter when purchasing a home that is not completed when you enter the agreement to buy it is that of co-ordinating the date of completion of the construction of the home with your date of occupancy. If this is not done properly, two problems can occur.

First, you usually have to make arrangements to move well in advance of the scheduled occupancy date and you have probably either sold your home with a similar possession date or you have made a commitment to give up your lease. You then find yourself in a situation where you have to move out of your old home or apartment but you have no place to move into, since the new home is not yet ready to accommodate you. This is compounded by the legalities that usually accompany the situation — in the new house that you are purchasing, the vendor usually has the right to postpone the closing but in the house that you are selling or in the apartment from which you are moving, you will usually face liability if you don't move. There is a further compounding factor related to this problem which is the reality that many new homes are bought many months, sometimes more than a year, before the construction can be completed — in the interim, there can be many matters beyond the control of the builder (e.g., problems encountered with the subdivider, servicing, labor strikes, shortage of material, etc.) that cause the acutal moving date to occur many weeks or months after the date originally anticipated. There is more on this last point a little later in this section.

Second, if you choose to take possession of the new house because you have nowhere else to go even though it is uncompleted (assuming that construction has reached the stage that will allow you to occupy the new house), the builder will probably insist that the entire purchase price be paid before you are allowed to move in. You are then left in the situation where you will have to depend on the builder's continued financial solvency and integrity to complete the remaining items of construction in a proper manner and within a reasonable period of time. This can cause major problems for you.

Suppose, for example, there are several items of construction that must be completed after you have paid your money, but the builder, before being able to complete them, goes into bankruptcy. In this situation, you are faced with the problem of having to get another contractor to do the first contractor's work and, in essence, you end up paying two people to do the same work.

One very important clause in most (and probably all) builders' standard forms of agreement of purchase and sale is that a builder may postpone the date of possession. This clause is necessary for the builder to have flexibility in the timing of the completion of the construction of the house. The rationale is that since the builder does not have control over strikes, availability of supplies, weather conditions, subdivider's obligations and the like, there should be a provision in the agreement of purchase and sale that allows the builder to postpone the date of closing. In most situations where a reasonable purchaser is dealing with a reasonable and reputable builder, which is the usual situation, there would be no need to say anything further. However, events reported in the newspapers during 1985 and 1986 have brought about legislated changes in this area. First, purchasers were experiencing long delays in their completion dates, sometimes in excess of a year. The difficulty of finding temporary accommodation for a long period of time combined with the uncertainty of not knowing if the house would ever be completed, made life difficult for many purchasers caught in the middle of the situation, even when the cause of the delay was something entirely out of the control of the builder. Second, the clause giving the builder the right to postpone the closing was often combined with a right in favor of the builder to terminate the agreement of purchase and sale if construction was not completed within a specified time after the originally anticipated closing date (e.g., 90 days). In a market where house prices are escalating, builders of questionable morality were said to be purposely delaying closing dates in order to avail themselves of the right to terminate the agreement of purchase and sale with the first purchaser so that they could turn around and sell the same house to another purchaser (or even the same purchaser) at a higher price. In the winter of 1986-87, the Ontario government announced plans to pass legislation to remedy this problem. However, as of April, 1987, this legislation had not been introduced. Instead (and, perhaps, as we shall see as time passes, in addition), the Ontario New Home Warranty Program, after consultation with several groups interested in the new home industry, including the Ministry of Housing of the Ontario government, made a change in their requirements of builders. As of March 2, 1987, a builder must disclose to each purchaser certain information, including that the agreement of purchase and sale may contain provisions by which the builder may terminate the agreement, regardless of whether or not the purchaser is in default, that the purchaser is advised to consult a solicitor before signing the agreement, the planning status of the property (i.e., whether the plan of subdivision is or is not registered and whether a building permit is or is not available) and the following clauses are incorporated into the agreement of purchase and sale:

(i) If the Vendor cannot close the transaction by the closing date in the Agreement because additional time is required for construction of the dwelling, the Vendor shall extend the closing date one or more times as may be required by the Vendor by notice in writing to the Purchaser as soon as reasonably possible and in any event prior to the closing date or extended closing date, all extensions in the aggregate not to exceed 120 days. However, the Vendor shall not extend closing if the parties have specifically agreed in writing that the Vendor cannot, and the Purchaser does not waive this covenant.

(ii) The Vendor shall take all reasonable steps to construct the dwelling without delay.

The Ontario New Home Warranty Program is attempting to make purchasers better informed as to the status of their transaction and to provide them with the right to terminate their agreement of purchase and sale if closing does not occur within 120 days after that originally anticipated. It remains to be seen whether these provisions, either alone or in conjunction with other changes in the law or practice, will achieve the desired result.

In addition to the foregoing changes, it is strongly suggested that you consider the following to protect yourself:

(a) When closing dates are discussed for the purpose of the agreement of purchase and sale, get an estimate from the builder as to when the house is expected to be ready, add some time to that estimate to provide a margin of error and delete the clause permitting the builder to postpone closing. This will not be agreeable to many builders and will be unacceptable to any builder in times when the market for the sale of homes is quite good.

(b) Attempt to obtain agreement with the builder as to what will happen if the house is not completed. For example, if the house is not completed by the closing date, try to have the builder pay the cost of storage of furniture, pay some portion of the purchaser's cost for renting temporary accommodation, have the builder provide a model home or a home that is not sold with payment of the moving costs from the temporary home to the new home when it has been completed, provide for a holdback, etc. As in (a) above, in a market that is good for builders, builders will likely not even consider anything of this nature. However, if the market for homes is not strong for builders, some builders will entertain discussion of dealing with this concern in ways that they would not consider in better times. The concept of a holdback is that a specified amount or an amount determined in a specified manner could be held in trust by either the builder's or purchaser's lawyer and not released until the lawyer receives permission from both parties or is given satisfactory proof that the items agreed upon have been completed and if these items are not completed within a specified time, the purchaser would have the right to have someone else complete construction with the holdback being used to pay this other contractor.

Depending on the market conditions and the particular builder's attitude, there may or may not be any room for negotiation of anything in the builder's agreement, including the price. Many builders have had their agreements specially prepared to suit their circumstances and feel that the prospective purchaser must either accept or reject the form. Here it can only be suggested that if you ask for something that is reasonable and the builder adopts the "take it or leave it" attitude, it may very well be your first warning of storm clouds ahead — so watch out!

3. Subdivision agreement
In addition to all the aforementioned problems, you should be aware of a "subdivision agreement." A subdivider (developer) of the land is usually required to enter into a subdivision agreement with the municipality in which the land is located before beginning to develop raw acreage into building lots. The major purpose of the subdivision agreement is to provide for the installation and payment of

services, such as water supply, storm sewers, sanitary sewers, roadways and sidewalks. In order to make all future owners of the property aware of the provisions of the subdivision agreement, it is common for the municipality to register a copy of the agreement on the title to the property. When a subdivision agreement is encountered during the title search of a new home, it will be necessary to obtain the various clearances from the municipality. This, of course, is the responsibility of the purchaser's legal advisor. The subdivision agreement not only provides for the installation and payment of municipal services but also provides certain standards which must be met by the builder.

Thus, the municipality through this agreement attempts to assist prospective home owners by requiring them to compel the builder to complete the premises prior to the transfer of possession. However, this is more true in theory than in practice because many purchasers are faced with the practical problem of requiring possession at a specific time and, accordingly, instead of relying on the non-occupancy prohibitions in the subdivision agreement, the purchaser will accept all of the risks involved in moving into an uncompleted home. In this situation, if the municipality wishes to stringently enforce this type of non-occupancy prohibition, the hardship will be placed on the purchaser, rather than on the builder for whom it was intended.

It is possible to protect yourself against this potential hardship and we would suggest that you should discuss this matter with your lawyer before signing an offer to purchase.

The specific provisions of the various subdivision agreements in common use today differ from municipality to municipality and, of course, if the agreement has been complied with, it is usually not necessary or important for the purchaser to be aware of its provisions.

4. Zoning
The purpose of zoning by-laws is to govern the orderly development of the community. The zoning by-laws

regulate and govern, among other things, the use the building may be put to, the type of building that may be constructed, and the set back — that is, the required distance between the house and the lot lines.

Such regulations provide that all homes in the area will conform to the planning principles laid down by the municipal authorities. Again, if you are in doubt about whether the home being purchased, new or old, conforms to the local zoning by-laws, you can easily verify it by contacting the appropriate municipal authorities. This should be done especially if any alterations or additions to the home are planned.

5. Contracting to build a new home

Instead of buying a home from a builder, you may wish to have a home built to your specifications. Should this be the case, you should choose the contractor carefully and give considerable thought to that contractor's reputation. A construction agreement is of paramount importance, but it should be remembered that a contract is only as good as the people who make it. Ideally, a construction contract should be tailor-made to a specific job in order to cover specifically what must be done.

There are, however, some common elements applicable to most construction contracts and to which some thought should be given before you enter into discussions with a builder. They are as follows:

(a) The date of the agreement and an accurate definition of the parties

(b) An accurate description of the work to be done by the contractor

(c) The time of commencement and completion of the work

(d) Damages in case the completion date is not met (This should be an honest estimate of the damages; otherwise it will not stand up in court.)

(e) The price and terms of payment

(f) Consideration of a performance bond

(g) Warranties that the work will be performed in a competent manner and that all materials will be new

(h) Clarification of whose responsibility it shall be to pay for and obtain permits, licences, and connection fees

(i) Particulars of fire and liability insurance to be carried on the project

(j) Provision for the contractor to obtain written approval by the owner before extra costs and additional work are incurred

(k) Provisions to correct and remedy defects in workmanship and material for a certain period of time, as well as a provision setting out the owner's alternative if there is a breach of contract

(l) A provision by the builder to protect the owner against construction lien claims

(m) A provision that the builder and that builder's subtrades abide by all laws

(n) A provision requiring the contractor to clean up after the job is completed

(o) A provision for settling disputes by arbitration (optional)

(p) A standard provision stating that the contract contains the entire agreements unless altered in writing

(q) A provision indicating that time is of the essence.

(r) A provision stating how a notice is to be given to the parties under the contract should'it be required

(s) A provision indicating the agreement is binding on the heirs and successors of the parties.

6. Construction Lien Act

In 1983, the Construction Lien Act replaced the Mechanics' Lien Act. This new act applies to contractors, subcontractors, material suppliers and other people involved in developing real estate.

The Construction Lien Act is an important consideration for anybody purchasing a new home, doing additional construction on an existing home, or renovating a home. The act obliges an owner to withhold from the contractor or subcontractor an amount equal to 10% of the price of the services or materials until all liens have been satisfied. In addition, the Construction Lien Act imposes a trust on all amounts received that are to be used in the financing of the work.

The holdback must be retained for 45 days after "substantial performance" of the contract. Substantial performance is determined by the procedure set out in the act and depends on the circumstances of the particular contract. Usually it relates to the time of certification or publication.

An owner who breaches these holdback requirements faces double payment. If a holdback is wrongly paid to one party, the owner of the property may have to pay the holdback to the correct party while being unable to recover it from the party to whom it was wrongly paid.

Additional protection, in the form of liability exemptions for liens, is available to a person who buys the interest of an owner in a home, whether built or not at the time of the agreement of purchase and sale. Certain provisions must be met for this exemption to be allowed. First, not more than 30% of the purchase price can be paid prior to the conveyance. Second, the home cannot be conveyed until it is ready for occupancy. The theory behind this exemption is that the protection of the person entitled to construction liens will be provided by the party who provides the 70% or more of the financing.

In order to protect yourself against liability under the act, provision can be made in the agreement of purchase and sale so that you, as purchaser, may reserve the right to retain the holdback for the required period of time. In all cases, when the holdback period has expired, a search should be made in the Land Registry Office to make sure that the property is free of liens. If there are any liens registered, contact your lawyer to make sure they are discharged before you pay out the holdback money. A mortgage company will not make progress advances until these liens are lifted to protect its own liabilities.

There are a number of ways of having construction liens discharged from a property, but suffice it to say that if you are involved in a situation where a construction lien is claimed, you should seek professional guidance immediately.

In addition to construction defects which could arise, a new home also contains new and untried systems, such as furnace and electrical systems. You should check into guarantees and warranties that may be available to you in addition to the warranty provided by the Ontario New Home Warranty Program (which used to be called the HUDAC Warranty), *before* you sign the agreement of purchase and sale. If there are any, it should be noted in the agreement that the purchaser is to receive an assignment of these warranties and guarantees on closing, if they are assignable.

7. Easements and rights-of-way

Easements and rights-of-way give certain people special rights for specific purposes regarding adjacent properties of others. While, in many cases, it is not necessary for an easement or right-of-way to be registered and to be shown on the search of title to the property, on a newly constructed house it will usually be registered.

Easements facilitate the provision of services such as hydro, telephone, water pipes, storm sewers, and sanitary sewers. In order to be of minimum inconvenience to the owner they are usually located along the side or at the rear of the lot lines of the property. The usual form of easement agreement gives authority to the parties indicated in the agreement to install, maintain, repair, and keep their lines of service in good condition throughout the easement. Most easement agreements also provide that the parties who maintain such services are under an obligation to restore the surface of the property to the same condition as it was prior to the installation or repair.

In addition to the foregoing, most easement agreements prohibit the owner of the property from building on top of the easement, whether it be an extensive renovation such as a pool or just a tool shed. If the rights of the owner of a right-of-way agreement or easement are infringed upon, that owner would have a right of action against the person who caused the infringement.

8. The Ontario New Home Warranty Program

The Ontario New Home Warranty Program was established by the Ontario New Homes Warranty Plan Act, 1976, to protect the purchasers of *new* homes (older homes and partially completed homes are not covered) against loss of deposit monies and against breaches of the vendor's warranty obligations.

When this program was originally introduced, the warranty was referred to as the HUDAC New Home Warranty because the administration of the program was undertaken by HUDAC, an association of housing builders and developers. It is for this reason that one still hears this warranty referred to as the "HUDAC Warranty." However, the administration of the warranty program is no longer taken care of by HUDAC and the name of the warranty and the warranty program has been changed. The administration of the warranty has always been and continues to be a non-governmental function, even though the establishment of the program was by way of Ontario legislation.

The basics of the program are as follows:

(a) Every vendor or builder, in order to be legally entitled to sell a new home in Ontario, must be registered with the Ontario New Home Warranty Program. In considering an application, Ontario New Home Warranty Program must be satisfied as to the applicant's financial position, past conduct and level of technical competence. Registration is valid for one year and may be renewed. The purpose of requiring annual registration is, of course, to prevent irresponsible builders from building homes and to weed out builders who demonstrate themselves to be irresponsible after a period of probation.

(b) You should be aware that not all aspects of construction are covered by this warranty. To find out exactly what is covered, you should refer to the actual warranty certificate, a specimen of which is available at local offices of the Ontario New Home Warranty Program. (See Appendix for a list of offices.)

The standards of construction are contained in the Building Code, established under the Building Code Act, 1974. The warranty is for a total of five years. During the first year, the builder is responsible for repairing defects in material and/or workmanship as set forth in the warranty certificate. The builder's responsibility then ceases. It is the responsibility of Ontario New Home Warranty Program to make sure that the builder fulfills the obligations during the first year and for the remainder of the five years of the warranty, to ensure that major structural defects in construction that would vitally affect the use of the home are repaired or resolved, to a maximum financial limit established and changed from time to time by the Ontario government. The program has established a guarantee fund against which claims can be made. Many new home buyers have, unfortunately, found that they are unable to obtain help from Ontario New Home Warranty Program because their complaint is not made in time — one year after the closing date.

(c) All claims are made against Ontario New Home Warranty Program and not the builder. Personnel will be provided by Ontario New Home Warranty Program to conduct conciliation proceedings within the framework provided in the legislation to resolve certain disputes between the purchaser and the builder.

There are two important precautions that should be stressed. First, know what the warranty provides and what you must do to protect your rights under the warranty. Ask your local office. Second, prior to taking possession of the home you will be asked to sign a certificate of completion and possession which is filed with Ontario New Home Warranty Program. This certificate forms the basis of the builder's obligations during the first year of the warranty by listing all defects in construction at that point in time. No matter how minor the problem is and regardless of the builder's promises to repair or finish the work, *all* unsatisfactory items of construction should be listed. If the builder will not sign your list, keep it and refuse to sign the certificate containing the builder's list — and report the events in writing to the Ontario New Home Warranty Program for their files.

The Ontario New Home Warranty Program has shown itself to be anxious to provide the general public, both builders and purchasers alike, with information and it will provide pamphlets and other types of information upon request.

d. BUYING AN OLDER HOME

1. General

Many of the things that are applicable to buying a new home are also applicable to the purchase of an older home and vice versa. The term "older home" here refers to a home that has been previously occupied whether or not the home is less than one year old or more than fifty.

There are certain disadvantages to buying an older home. You could be buying somebody else's problems, such as a leaky roof, pests, or other items that need attention. On the other hand, the landscaping will probably be done and so will that recreation room in the basement, which is usually unfinished in a new home. Similarly, many details such as the screen and storm doors and that extra carpet have probably also been installed. These seemingly little items could add up to a big expense if you had to do them.

As most Canadians move seven times in their lifetime, the age of the home may not be a factor. In any event, it is a personal decision which revolves around monetary and "life style" factors.

2. Warranties, representations, and inspections

When you are buying an older home it is obvious that many questions should be asked and satisfactory answers obtained before an offer to purchase is made. What is not obvious is that you can do a great deal to protect yourself by making sure your offer to purchase contains these warranties and representations in writing. The most important of these could be inserted in the offer as conditions to be met *before* the transaction is closed. Sample #2 is an example of an offer to purchase that has been signed by all parties and is now an agreement of purchase and sale. Please note that it is included only as a sample and is not intended to illustrate the ultimate in protection for a purchaser, for what is important to one purchaser may not be important to another.

If you are not sure what you are doing, it is far better for you to spend a small amount at this point in obtaining expert advice from a lawyer or someone else familiar with the real estate business than a large amount later trying to get out of a bad deal.

This technique of reducing the important representations to writing in the offer is an excellent way of flushing out potential problems. If, for example, the vendor is asked to make certain warranties and representations in the offer and signs it as having accepted it, that vendor is then legally committed. If, however, the vendor crosses out an item in the offer, you are being alerted to a potential problem and you can then pursue the matter and make further inquiries.

It goes without saying that you should carefully inspect the house before submitting an offer. As a matter of fact, and as previously mentioned, it is a good idea to inspect the house a minimum of three times, preferably once on a sunny day, once on a rainy day, and once at night.

Visual inspection of the house will reveal water stains, the condition of the painting, plastering, carpets, lights and light fixtures, etc. It will not reveal, however, whether certain other items will require repair — such as the roof, furnace, hot water tank, or the condition of the electrical, plumbing, and heating systems. Problems with any of these could be very costly.

In some areas commercial house inspection services exist. We highly recommend spending the $100 to $200 to take advantage of such a service. In addition, there are several homeowners' associations that will provide inspection services for members. There are also several private consulting and inspection firms.

When considering the cost of the house, such an inspection is worthwhile. If there is no commercial inspection service in your area, it is highly recommended that you contact someone knowledgeable in home construction and pay that person to look the house over thoroughly and have the place inspected for pests.

Also keep in mind that you may want to take measurements in your new home for such things as drapes, painting estimates, appliance installation and the purchase of broadloom and furniture. In addition, you may wish to satisfy yourself that the house is in the same condition at closing as it was when you signed the agreement of purchase and sale.

The right of inspection prior to closing should be considered in every residential real estate purchase. The right of a purchaser to inspect a home between the time of signing the agreement of purchase and sale and the time of closing is not an automatic right. In fact, if you wish to enter the home prior to the closing of the transaction, a clause to this effect must be included in the agreement.

This provision should specify the manner in which the right of inspection may be exercised. For example, a right of inspection may specify that the purchaser has a right to inspect the dwelling during any evening between the hours of 5:00 p.m. and 7:00 p.m. after providing to the vendor 24 hours written notice and that this right of inspection extends to the purchaser and any tradesmen employed by the purchaser.

A county court decision held in one case that an agreement of purchase and sale that did not contain the right of inspection but did contain the standard clause that the property was to remain at the risk of vendor until closing,

SAMPLE #2
AGREEMENT OF PURCHASE AND SALE
(Older Home)

FOR USE IN THE PROVINCE OF ONTARIO

Toronto Real Estate Board

AGREEMENT OF PURCHASE AND SALE

PURCHASER. PETER PURCHASER .... offers to buy from

VENDOR. VERNA VENDOR and VICTOR VENDOR .... through Vendor's

AGENT. CONSCIENTIOUS REAL ESTATE .... the following

PROPERTY: fronting on the NORTH .... side of ANY STREET ....

known municipally as 1234 ANY STREET .... in the CITY .... of TORONTO ....

and having a frontage of 15.85 METRES ...... more or less by a depth of 33.5 METRES ...... more or less and described as ....

.... a fully detached brick and stucco dwelling house having a private driveway ....

.... and single garage ....

at the PURCHASE PRICE of EIGHTY NINE THOUSAND NINE HUNDRED ------------------------------------

CANADIAN DOLLARS ($ CAN 89,900.00 ---) payable on the following terms:

1 PURCHASER submits with this Offer FIVE THOUSAND FOUR HUNDRED ----------------- DOLLARS ($ 5,400.00----),
payable by cash/cheque to the Vendor's Agent as a deposit to be held by him in trust pending completion or other termination of this Agreement and to be
credited on account of the purchase price on closing; and

2 PURCHASER agrees to: pay a further sum of ELEVEN THOUSAND SIX HUNDRED DOLLARS ($11 600.00),
subject to the usual adjustments by cash or certified cheque on closing.

Purchaser agrees to assume an existing first mortgage having a balance of about
$44 800.00, bearing interest at the rate of 12% per annum, calculated half-yearly, not
in advance, repayable in equal blended montly instalments of $474.68, which includes
both principal and interest and matures on June 30, 198–.

On closing, Purchaser shall give and Vendor shall take back a second mortgage
for the balance of the purchase price, bearing interest at the rate of 9% per annum,
repayable in quarterly instalments of $100.00 on account of principal plus interest,
having a term of 3 years and containing a privilege whereby the Purchaser may prepay
the whole or any part of the principal sum at any time or times without notice or
bonus.

SCHEDULE "A" ATTACHED HERETO FORMS A PART OF THIS AGREEMENT.

3. PURCHASER AND VENDOR agree that all existing fixtures are included in the purchase price except those listed hereunder:
CHANDELIER IN DINING ROOM.

and that the following chattels are included in the purchase price: All electric light fixtures, all storm and screen
windows and doors, broadloom where laid, washer, dryer, dishwasher, refrigerator, stove,
drapes, drapery tracks and fireplace equipment now on the property and belonging to
Vendor free of encumbrances.

4. PURCHASER agrees that this Offer shall be irrevocable by him until 11:59 p.m. on the 11th day of June 19 8–
after which time, if not accepted, this Offer shall be null and void and the deposit shall be returned to Purchaser without interest or deduction.

5. THIS AGREEMENT shall be completed on the 31st day of July 19 8– Upon completion, vacant
possession of the property shall be given to Purchaser unless otherwise provided as follows.

6. PURCHASER shall be allowed the 30 days next following the date of acceptance of this Offer to: examine the title to the property at his own expense, to
satisfy himself that there are no outstanding municipal work orders or deficiency notices affecting the property, that its present use
(residential) may be lawfully continued, and that the principal building may be insured against risk of fire. Vendor hereby consents to the
municipality releasing to Purchaser details of all outstanding municipal work orders or deficiency notices affecting the property.

7. VENDOR AND PURCHASER agree that there is no condition, express or implied, representation or warranty of any kind that the future intended use of the property by Purchaser is or will be lawful except as may be specifically stipulated hereunder.

8. PURCHASER acknowledges having inspected the property prior to submitting this Offer and understands that upon Vendor accepting this Offer there shall be a
binding agreement of purchase and sale between Purchaser and Vendor.

Form No. 001 (83/05)

45

9. PROVIDED THAT the title to the property is good and free from all encumbrances except for any registered restrictions or covenants that run with the land providing that such are complied with and except for any minor easements for the supply of domestic utility services to the property. If within the time allowed for examining the title any valid objection to title, or to any outstanding municipal work order or deficiency notice, or to the fact the said present use may not lawfully be continued, or that the principal building may not be insured against risk of fire is made in writing to Vendor and which Vendor is unable or unwilling to remove, remedy or satisfy and which Purchaser will not waive, this Agreement notwithstanding any intermediate acts or negotiations in respect of such objections, shall be at an end and all monies theretofore paid shall be returned without interest or deduction and Vendor and Vendor's Agent shall not be liable for any costs or damages. Save as to any valid objection so made by such day and except for any objection going to the root of the title, Purchaser shall be conclusively deemed to have accepted Vendor's title to the property.

10. PURCHASER shall not call for the production of any title deed, abstract, survey or other evidence of title to the property except such as are in the possession or control of Vendor. Vendor agrees that he will deliver any sketch or survey of the property in his possession or within his control to Purchaser as soon as possible and prior to the last day allowed for examining title.

11. ALL buildings on property and all other things being purchased shall be and remain until completion at the risk of Vendor. Pending completion, Vendor shall hold all insurance policies, if any, and the proceeds thereof in trust for the parties as their interest may appear and in the event of substantial damage, Purchaser may either terminate this Agreement and have all monies theretofore paid returned without interest or deduction or else take the proceeds of any insurance and complete the purchase.

12. PROVIDED THAT this Agreement shall be effective to create an interest in the property only if the subdivision control provisions of the Planning Act are complied with by Vendor on or before completion and the Vendor hereby covenants to proceed diligently at his expense to obtain any necessary consent on or before completion.

13. VENDOR shall, on completion, deliver sufficient proof that the property is not a matrimonial home within the meaning of the Family Law Reform Act or otherwise comply with provisions thereof.

14. PURCHASER shall be credited towards the Purchase Price with the amount, if any, which it shall be necessary for Purchaser to pay to the Receiver General of Canada in order to satisfy Purchaser's liability in respect of tax payable by Vendor under the non-residency provisions of the Income Tax Act by reason of this sale. Purchaser shall not claim such credit if Vendor delivers on completion the prescribed certificate or his statutory declaration that he is not then a non-resident of Canada.

15. VENDOR shall supply to Purchaser at least five (5) days before completion details of any fire insurance to be assigned on closing.

16. UNEARNED FIRE INSURANCE PREMIUMS, rents, mortgage interest, taxes, local improvement, water and assessment rates and the cost of fuel shall be apportioned and allowed to the day of completion (the day itself to be apportioned to Purchaser).

17. THE deed or transfer shall, save for the Land Transfer Tax Affidavits, be prepared in registrable form at the expense of Vendor and the Mortgage at the expense of Purchaser.

18. TIME shall in all respects be of the essence hereof provided that the time for doing or completing of any matter provided for herein may be extended or abridged by an agreement in writing signed by Vendor and Purchaser or by their respective solicitors who are hereby expressly appointed in this regard.

19. ANY TENDER of documents or money hereunder may be made upon Vendor or Purchaser or their respective solicitors on the day for completion of this Agreement. Money may be tendered by bank draft or cheque certified by a chartered bank, trust company or Province of Ontario Savings Office.

20. THIS AGREEMENT shall constitute the entire agreement between Purchaser and Vendor and there is no representation, warranty, collateral agreement or condition affecting this Agreement or the property or supported hereby other than as expressed herein in writing. This Agreement shall be read with all changes of gender or number required by the context.

DATED at Toronto .... this 10th day of June 19 8-

SIGNED, SEALED AND DELIVERED)
in the presence of)
)   IN WITNESS whereof I have hereunto set my hand and seal
)
)
)   (Affix Seal)   (Date)
)   (Purchaser)
)
)
)   (Affix Seal)   (Date)
)   (Purchaser)

THE UNDERSIGNED accepts the above Offer and agrees with the Agent above named in consideration for his services in procuring the said offer, to pay him on the date above fixed for completion, a commission of six (6) % of an amount equal to the above mentioned sale price, which commission may be deducted from the deposit. I hereby irrevocably instruct my solicitor to pay direct to the Agent any unpaid balance of commission from the proceeds of the sale.

DATED AT Toronto .... this 10th day of June 19 8-

SIGNED, SEALED AND DELIVERED)
in the presence of)
)   IN WITNESS whereof I have hereunto set my hand and seal
)
)
)   (Affix Seal)   (Date)
)   (Vendor)
)
)   (Affix Seal)   (Date)
)   (Vendor)

ACKNOWLEDGEMENT

I acknowledge receipt of my signed copy of this accepted Agreement of Purchase and Sale

I acknowledge receipt of my signed copy of this accepted Agreement of Purchase and Sale

(Vendor)   (Date)   (Purchaser)   (Date)

(Vendor)   (Date)   (Purchaser)   (Date)

Vendor's Address   Purchaser Address

Telephone No.   Telephone No.

Vendor's Solicitor   Purchaser's Solicitor

Solicitor's Address   Solicitor's Address

Telephone No.   Telephone No.

SCHEDULE "A"
To Agreement of Purchase and Sale between Peter Purchaser, as Purchaser, and
Verna Vendor and Victor Vendor, as Vendors, dated June 10th, 198 for the
property known as 1234 Any Street, Toronto.

1.   The Vendors warrant and represent that the real property has not been
insultated with Urea Formaldehyde Foam Insulation, such warranty and
representation to survive the closing of this transaction.

2.   The Vendors covenant and agree as follows:

a)   That they will provide to the Purchaser or his solicitors a survey of
the real property within 15 days of the date of acceptance hereof,
which survey was prepared at or about the time of purchase of the real
property by the Vendors;

b)   That the Purchaser shall have the right to inspect the real property
during daylight hours until the closing of the within transaction, upon
providing to the Vendors 24 hours prior notice of his intention so to
inspect;

3.   It is a condition of the completion of the within transaction by the
Purchaser as follows:

a)   That the dwelling on the real property has been constructed in
accordance with all relevant municipal, provincial and federal
requirements;

b)   That the heating system, plumbing system, electrical system and roof
are not in need of repair. The Purchaser shall have the right to have
the plumbing system, heating system, electrical system and roof
inspected by his agents or contractors prior to closing;

c)   That there are no easements, rights of way or encroachments of any kind
whatsoever affecting the real property, save and except for an easement
in favour of Bell Canada and the Hydro Electric Commission of the City
of Toronto, which easement is located along the rear six (6) feet of
the real property.

4.   It is understood and agreed as follows:

a)   That the upstairs flat at the real property is rented to Tom Tenant on
a month-to-month tenancy (no written lease) at a monthly rent of
$150.00 per month payable, in advance, on the 1st day of each and
every month;

b)   The Purchaser shall have the right to move his furniture and chattel
property onto the real property during the seven day period prior to
closing and this right shall in no way derogate from any of the other
rights of the Purchaser under the within agreement or at law. The
Vendors shall not be responsible for loss or damage to the property of
the Purchaser occurring in any way whatsoever.

concluded that the latter clause entitled the purchaser to inspect the property immediately prior to closing in order to satisfy himself that there had been no damage to the property. This decision was not appealed to a high court and was based upon the specific wording of the contract and circumstances of that case. We do not recommend that a purchaser rely on this decision to obtain a right of inspection. However, if a right of inspection has been omitted from the agreement of purchase and sale, this decision may be helpful in obtaining a right of inspection prior to closing.

3. Work orders

Many municipalities have enacted by-laws to establish minimum housing standards. These housing standards are legislated for the benefit of home owners in order to ensure that all houses in the municipality meet minimum requirements of safety. The usual manner of operation of these housing standard by-laws is for the municipality to issue a "work order" if the home owner is in breach of any of the provisions of a by-law.

A work order is a document directed to the home owner that the house is in breach of the by-law and requires the home owner to repair the deficiency. You, or your lawyer, should make a search at the proper municipality to see if there are outstanding or pending work orders affecting the property.

Most standard form offers to purchase now incorporate a clause concerning work orders. This clause is the same clause that allows a certain period of time to the purchaser for the purpose of inspecting title. If, during this time, the purchaser becomes aware of any outstanding work orders for the property, the purchaser may, if the purchaser feels that the work order is of substantial cost, cancel the agreement of purchase and sale and receive a return of his or her deposit.

There are two things you should be aware of about this procedure:
(a) The number of days usually inserted into the offer is quite short (usually 20 or 30 days), and this often

does not give the purchaser or his or her lawyer sufficient time to find out from the municipality if there are any outstanding work orders.

(b) Since both vendor and purchaser will wish to make arrangements concerning their old and new homes, it would be prudent for both to await the outcome of the search of outstanding work orders. But, to wait for this extra time is usually not satisfactory for either of them, since they will both want to finalize all of their affairs as soon as possible after this deal is made.

There is a better way to handle this matter. The vendor, who has lived in the house for a period of time and is aware of the condition of the house, should know whether there are any outstanding work orders on file. It is, therefore, not unreasonable for the purchaser to insist upon the following conditions in the agreement of purchase and sale:

(a) If there are any work orders on file at the time of signing the agreement of purchase and sale, the vendor must, prior to closing, do the work necessary to satisfy these work orders so that the municipality will release them.

(b) If any work orders are issued between the time of signing the agreement of purchase and sale and the closing, the vendor has the right (but not the obligation) to satisfy the work orders before closing. The vendor will usually wish to comply with minor work orders in this fashion in order to close the transaction.

(c) If work orders arise between the time of signing the agreement of purchase and sale and the date of closing, and if the vendor is unable or unwilling to satisfy them before closing, the purchaser has the right to either accept the property and repair the work orders at his or her own expense after closing or to cancel the transaction. In this way, a serious work order will not place the vendor or the purchaser in a default situation with respect to each other, but will allow for the transaction to close-if the parties are so inclined. If the work order is serious and the transaction is cancelled, the vendor has the opportunity to appeal the work order or make other arrangements that do not affect the transaction.

It is important to remember that the work order clearance given by the municipality does not mean that there are no infractions of the appropriate by-laws. It is possible that there are infractions that have not been inspected or recorded on the files of the municipality.

4. Easements

In very old homes, utility easements are not common. However, in these homes there is always the possibility of easements, rights of way or encroachments having been granted for purposes other than utility easements and accordingly, you should check it out before submitting the offer to purchase. If there are any problems along this line, they should be described in detail in the offer to purchase. Normally, the purchaser is willing to accept title subject to these easements, rights of way or encroachments, but he or she should at least be aware of them. (See page 132 for more information.)

An example of this is as follows. Many older homes do not contain a driveway on the property limits, but rather, contain a driveway that is shared with the owner of the neighboring property. This driveway is commonly called a "mutual driveway." A mutual driveway is formed by neighbors granting to each other a common right of way over a specific portion of their property. For example, if a mutual driveway of 5 metres in width is required, each neighbor may contribute a strip of land 2 1/2 metres in width over which he or she grants to the neighbor the right of passage and, in turn, receives a similar right-of-way from this neighbor. Like an easement, a right-of-way cannot be built upon or impeded with to the detriment of the other party involved.

5. A survey

A survey is a drawing of a property prepared by an Ontario land surveyor as of a certain date (see Sample #3). The survey indicates the location of the boundaries of the property and any easements, rights of way or encroachments that affect the title to the property.

The survey of a new house will usually be prepared after the foundation is constructed and, therefore, will not show the completed dwelling. A survey is an important document in the purchase of a home for several reasons.

When you inspect a property, the boundaries of the property are not visible but, rather, are described in words in a deed or transfer. In order to translate these words into something that is visible, a survey is required which indicates the location of the boundaries of the property in relation to such things as the street line, fence lines and the walls of the dwelling on the property.

It is not uncommon for a vendor to honestly believe that the boundaries of the property are different from those described in the deed. Therefore, unless a survey is shown to the prospective purchaser, the erroneous understanding of the vendor may be passed on. In addition, fences are often not located directly on the property lines thus creating a mistaken impression as to the area of ownership.

There are many questions which may be answered by inspection of the survey. First, a survey will indicate the location of the boundaries and the actual area of property being purchased.

Second, a survey inspection will determine whether or not the fence lines are either on or within the boundaries of the property. If the fences have been erected outside of the boundary lines, and are on neighboring property, you, the purchaser, may be subjecting yourself to legal action by one of the neighbors for using property that is not yours.

Third, a survey will show if the property is encroached upon by neighboring lands or if it encroaches upon neighboring lands.

SAMPLE #3
SURVEY

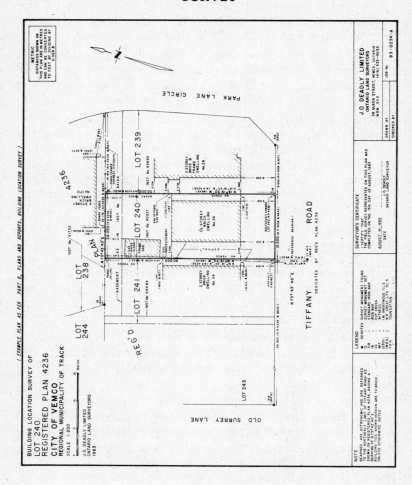

An encroachment is the use of one's property in such a way that it interferes with the use of another person's property in any way. An example of an encroachment is the overhanging of an eavestrough onto the neighbor's property, which might prevent the neighbor from building a structure on or near the lot line. Even if there are no buildings close to your neighbor's lot, an encroachment may exist, such as an encroachment over a right-of-way or over a setback in the zoning law.

The fourth and perhaps the most important reason for inspecting a survey is to make sure that the dwelling and the accessory buildings, such as the garage, tool shed, etc., are located entirely within the boundaries of the land being purchased. Again, a survey will inform you of a potential lawsuit by one of your neighbors for interfering with the use of this neighbor's lands.

A fifth reason for inspecting a survey is to determine the location of any easements or rights of way in existence over the property. This is important because if any construction has been done on an easement or right-of-way, the person who has the benefit of the use of the easement may have a right of action enforceable in a court of law. Locating an easement in relation to the positioning of fences may be erroneous if the fences do not coincide with the boundaries of the property.

The date of the last survey is an important matter to note because if changes have been made after the date of the survey, the survey, of course, will not be accurate. If the survey is dated when the vendor obtained title to the property, the vendor will be in full knowledge of all of the changes that have taken place to the property since the last survey. This should help you pinpoint possible problem areas. But you still should employ a surveyor to either prepare a new survey or to up-date the current survey to the time of the purchase.

The cost of either up-dating the survey or having a new survey prepared is a worthwhile investment. The new survey will enable you to be absolutely positive that there are no problems with regard to boundaries, location of buildings, easements or encroachments.

e. WHAT HAPPENS TO YOUR DEPOSIT?

When the sale is conducted through a real estate broker, the deposit is usually paid to the broker and is held in a trust account pending completion. In other words, the broker cannot legally touch the funds in any way until the deal is completed or until written authorization is given by both the vendor and purchaser or until a court order is obtained.

If the deal is not completed through no fault of the purchaser, he or she will usually be entitled to the return of the deposit. However, in cases where a purchaser provides a substantial deposit, or if a deposit is made directly to the vendor or if the purchaser has doubts as to the honesty of the vendor or the agent, the purchaser may wish to register a lien or claim against the property.

Both the Registry Act and the Land Titles Act provide a procedure for the registration of notice of such an interest.

Under the Registry Act, the purchaser would register a notice of the agreement of purchase and sale and, under the Land Titles Act, the purchaser would register an application with the agreement of purchase and sale attached. Both of these documents, when registered, provide notice to any person who subsequently searches the title of the property that the vendor has executed an agreement of purchase and sale and that the purchaser has a lien against the property for the amount of the deposit. Both of these documents must be renewed in order to continue to remain an outstanding claim.

Prior to registering this type of notice, the purchaser should review the agreement of purchase and sale, particularly when there is a builder's form involved, in order to ascertain that there is no prohibition against the registration of these interests.

The agreement of purchase and sale, especially a form that is prepared by a builder's lawyer, may provide that the registration of a notice will make the agreement of purchase and sale null and void and that the purchaser will forfeit the deposit.

The Ontario New Home Warranties Plan Act provides for the issuance of a deposit receipt by the vendor when a new house is purchased. This allows a purchaser to obtain compensation if he or she has a claim against a vendor for loss of deposit because the vendor went bankrupt, or because the vendor failed to perform the contract. Under this plan, you can claim from the guarantee fund to a maximum of $20 000.

f. CAN YOU HAVE TENANTS?

Many people purchase a larger home than their current requirements demand on the basis that they can rent out a portion of the premises. The reasoning behind this is that by buying a larger home at a slightly larger cost, the purchaser will subsequently be able to recover at least this extra cost from the tenant. In addition, after a number of years, if the purchaser wishes to expand his or her own dwelling unit, it will be possible to take over the portion of the dwelling formerly rented.

If you are concerned about the legality of renting out a portion of the premises, you must consider the provisions of the relevant zoning by-laws. Most municipalities have enacted zoning by-laws which regulate the use of the land within the municipality. The zoning by-laws often restrict the use of residential property to single family purposes. If the renting of rooms is an important factor to you, you should provide in the agreement of purchase and sale that it is a condition of the completion of the transaction that a specific portion of the premises may be rented in accordance with the relevant zoning by-law.

If the vendor has leased a portion of the premises to a tenant and if the parties agree that the purchaser will take possession of the premises subject to the tenancy, this situation should be described in the agreement of purchase and sale. Any purchaser in this situation should ascertain the terms of the tenancy including whether or not the tenancy is on a written or verbal basis, the term of the lease or tenancy, the rental amount and whether or not the tenant has any further right to renew the tenancy. This information should be obtained prior to submitting the offer.

In addition, you should provide in the offer that the vendor will obtain from the tenant an acknowledgement of the terms of the tenancy signed by the tenant prior to the closing of the transaction. This will serve to avoid any potential disputes with the tenants.

g. WHAT ABOUT THE APPLIANCES?

In addition to the sale of the real estate, the vendor, on many occasions, wants to dispose of other items, such as the washer and dryer, stove and fridge, drapes and built-in dishwasher. The general rule is that if they are permanently attached to the land or building they automatically form part of the real property unless they are specifically excluded. These items include built-in dishwasher, built-in wall ovens, attached light fixtures, and attached mirrors. If they are moveable, they are not part of the property; this includes curtains (as opposed to drapery tracks that are usually permanently attached), fridges, and stoves. In order to avoid any dispute as to whether or not a specific item is part of the property or not, you should list in full detail all the items that are included in the offer.

4

SO YOU CAN'T AFFORD A FULLY DETACHED OR SEMI-DETACHED HOME
(Alternative Forms of Home Ownership)

a. INTRODUCTION

As a result of substantial demand for cheaper forms of housing, new types of home ownership have become popular — the condominium and the co-operative.

Condominium and co-operative home ownership are both designed to maximize the benefit of common facilities such as land and structural portions of the building, thereby creating savings for the home owners.

Before getting too far into a discussion of condominium and co-operative housing, one misconception needs to be cleared up. The words "condominium" and "co-operative" refer to types of legal structure and not to physical structure.

Many people think of a condominium or co-operative as ownership of an apartment or a townhouse. Condominium and co-operative ownership do apply to apartments and townhouses, but could be applied equally well to an office building, warehouse or summer cottage development (where each member owns a cottage absolutely and shares in the ownership of common facilities, such as the beaches, wharves, motor boats, recreational areas, etc.)

In both condominiums and co-operatives, a type of society is formed. Each member of the society has an exclusive right to the use of part of the property (your own unit) and each member has a share of the remainder of the property (the common elements) in common with all of the other members. Thus, each member has an exclusive right and a shared right.

In co-operative ownership, a company is formed and this company is the owner of the entire property. The various members of the project own shares in this company (their shared right) and enter a lease with the company for the specific dwelling unit (their exclusive right). When a co-operative project member wishes to leave the project, you must find someone to purchase your shares and take an assignment of your lease.

In a condominium project, the member obtains a deed or transfer to the specific dwelling unit (your exclusive right) and becomes a co-owner with all other members of the common elements (your shared right).

In a condominium, you receive a direct legal title to your rights (both exclusive and shared) whereas in a co-operative you receive these rights indirectly through a company.

The major difference between condominium ownership and co-operative ownership is a practical difference and relates to mortgage payments and realty tax payments.

In a co-operative project, since the company owns the property, there is only one mortgage and one realty assessment to which each member must contribute. If one member should default in his or her obligation to make mortgage or tax contributions, the other members must make up the default.

In a condominium, all of the members of the project have their own mortgage and tax assessment on their own ownership. If one member of the project is in default, the remaining members are not required to remedy the default in mortgage or tax payments.

The condominium has become a very popular concept in the residential real estate market. Co-operative projects are few and far between. Thus, for the purposes of this book, the condominium will be discussed in substantial detail while our discussion of the co-operative will be very limited.

In recent years, the popularity of the co-operative concept has increased. This is, in part, a result of the requirement of filing detailed structural and mechanical plans in order to register a condominium. These plans, with the necessary detail, are not always available for older properties and cannot be created. The developer who wishes to sell each unit, rather than the whole building, can only proceed by using the co-operative concept.

Furthermore, many municipalities have recently developed criteria (e.g., parking) for condominium projects that are greater than the same type of requirement for rental properties. A municipality may impose a requirement for a rental project to have 1.25 parking spaces for each apartment suite and a condominium apartment building to have 1.5 parking spaces for each residential suite.

If the use of the co-operative concept becomes more popular, the government of Ontario will undoubtedly consider legislation governing co-operatives.

b. HOW A CONDOMINIUM WORKS

Even though the condominium is a relatively recent development in Ontario, the sale of condominium units currently represents a very large proportion of the residential real estate market, particularly in urban areas. There are two reasons for the popularity of the condominium.

First, the total purchase price of the condominium unit is usually lower than other types of housing and, second, the amount of the down payment required to purchase a condominium unit is also lower.

The reason that these costs are lower is that a condominium, by its nature, is an ownership by a number of people who are each contributing toward the common cost of expensive items, such as the cost of land. By sharing these common costs, the total price of the dwelling unit can be decreased. Of course, when such costs are decreased, there is usually a corresponding decrease in the amount of *benefit* derived from the item. In other words, if 15 people purchase land upon which each owns a dwelling, the benefit for each of these 15 people from the land will be reduced in comparison to a situation where the same acreage was purchased by only four people.

In the same manner that the purchase price and the amount of the down payment required are reduced in a condominium project, the amount of money required to carry the other ownership costs is reduced through this type of community living. For example, in a condominium project of 50 units, it is cheaper for the corporation to negotiate a contract for snow removal with one company than for each of the unit owners to arrange to pay for his or her own snow removal.

Condominium ownership, being a type of community living, requires that certain rules and regulations be established to determine each member's rights and obligations toward the others. The ultimate purpose of each rule and regulation is to maximize the combined enjoyment of all unit owners and minimize the interference with the enjoyment of ownership by each individual unit owner.

In comparison to single family detached dwellings, condominium owners are living much closer together and, therefore, are more dependent on each other for various purposes. Accordingly, a condominium owner's rights are, of necessity, more restricted (and obligations toward neighbors are greater) than the rights of an owner of a detached or semi-detached dwelling.

The rights and obligations are contained in the Condominium Act, the declaration (the document that creates the legal status of condominium), the by-laws (the internal documents of the condominium corporation) and the rules and regulations. In the same way that a condominium project can be viewed as a type of society or community, the Condominium Act, the declaration, the by-laws and the rules and regulations can be viewed together as the total constitution governing the society or community.

Some aspects of each of these "constitutional" documents are discussed in turn.

1. The Condominium Act

The Condominium Act was originally enacted in 1967 and has been amended several times.

In general terms, the Condominium Act describes some basic rights and obligations of all of the people involved with the project, i.e., the builder, the unit owner, the condominium corporation, the mortgagee (lender) and the property manager.

The Condominium Act regulates the matters considered by the Ontario government to be of the greatest importance to the condominium project, including protection. The Condominium Act provides minimum requirements for certain matters considered basic and allows private enterprise to provide for other matters. For example, it provides certain basic statements that a declaration document *must* contain and, in addition, lists several other statements that the declaration may contain.

Some of the highlights of the latest revision to the Condominium Act (which is actually a re-enactment of the Condominium Act) are:

(a) A new type of by-law (a "special by-law") can now be passed. A "special by-law" is required to permit a condominium corporation to lease common elements or to grant easements through the common elements.

(b) Duties of the condominium corporation and provisions regarding legal actions are now a part of the Condominium Act. These matters were formerly covered in the by-laws.

(c) Decisions at members' meetings are to be made on the basis of one vote per unit. Formerly, many decisions were based upon a vote that was weighted in accordance with percentage of ownership of common elements, as set forth in the declaration.

(d) Condominium developers must turn over specified items to the condominium corporation at the time when the board of directors is elected after the developer ceases to own a majority of the units.

(e) Insurance requirements are expanded.

(f) By-laws can be passed by a 51% majority. Formerly, a 66-2/3% or higher majority was required.

(g) Rules and regulations made by the board must be circulated to be effective and any rules and regulations made by the board can be referred to a meeting of owners.

(h) The provisions concerning auditing of condominium financial statements have been expanded. This will cause increased common expenses but, on the other hand, the statements will be more reliable.

(i) Reserve funds (at least one) are mandatory and at least 10% of the common expenses are to be contributed to the reserve fund.

(j) A "cooling off" period of 10 days is now available to purchasers of condominium units from the developer.

(k) A condominium bureau is to be established to advise and assist the public in condominium matters; to assist in the resolution of disputes between the condominium corporation and unit owners or between two or more unit owners; to disseminate condominium information; and to assist in conducting educational courses for property management. Each condominium corporation (and, therefore, each unit owner) will be required to pay a fee to this bureau. This fee is based on the number of units in the project. In addition, each corporation will be required to file information (including financial reports) to the bureau.

(l) Agreements made when the developer is in control of the condominium corporation are ended after 12 months unless they are ratified by the board of directors which is elected after the developer ceases to be in control of the condominium corporation. This helps prevent "sweetheart deals" between the developer and a related management corporation.

(m) Workmanship and material warranties obtained by the condominium developer are available to the condominium corporation and the unit owners, so they may act on them.

(n) A maximum amount is established for interim occupancy (rent) payments required to be paid by a purchaser before getting title to the unit. This amount consists of the amount of mortgage interest the purchaser would have to pay if the purchaser's mortgage were in effect, the estimated monthly realty taxes and the estimated common expenses.

2. The declaration

A condominium cannot be established as a condominium until a declaration is registered on the title to the property.

Accordingly, the condominium declaration is one of the earliest documents to be prepared and registered. The declaration is probably the single most important document in a condominium project because the matters of the greatest importance to the unit owners are included in it.

The Condominium Act recognizes the importance of the declaration and provides that it cannot be amended unless the amending vote is carried unanimously by all of the unit owners and by all of the holders of encumbrances (mortgages). Some common restrictions on units may be as follows:

(a) Use of the unit as a single-family residential dwelling

(b) Prohibition against the keeping of certain types of pets

(c) Requirement of obtaining consent of the board of directors for any proposed change or alteration of a unit

(d) Requirement of placing garbage in a common garbage disposal area

(e) Prohibition against displaying signs or notices on any unit

(f) Requirement of the unit owners to deposit a key to the unit with the management organization, in order that the unit may be entered in the case of a fire or similar emergency. Many people view this provision as an unwarranted intrusion of privacy but, because of the close proximity of the owners and danger of damage to other units, it is a reasonable request as long as it is not abused by the manager.

As can be seen, the condominium declaration attempts to achieve a maximization of the combined interests of all unit owners while, at the same time, minimizing the infringement on the enjoyment of each individual owner. Sometimes this is easier said than done.

Because it provides for far-reaching restrictions, we strongly suggest that you read the declaration or the proposed declaration very thoroughly *before* submitting an offer to purchase. If there are objectionable restrictions, you may need legal advice.

Even though the "cooling off" period (now available to purchasers of new condominium units from the builder) provides some protection against a hasty decision, it is still important to know what you are getting into before signing. Furthermore, the cooling off period is not applicable to the resale of condominium units; the cooling off period is only for people who purchase new residential condominium units from the condominium developer.

One final note regarding the declaration is that many condominium declarations provide for a contingency fund. The purpose of a contingency fund is to assist the unit owners in coping with an unexpected emergency that would otherwise be a costly expenditure for all of them or to allow the condominium corporation to pay seasonally large expenses, such as heating.

3. The by-laws

The by-laws of a condominium project consider matters of lesser importance. Some of these matters are the internal operation of the condominium corporation, the holding of meetings, the board of directors, the officers of the condominium corporation, the duties and powers of the condominium corporation, the banking arrangements and the requirements of providing notice.

The Condominium Act now provides that the by-laws of the condominium corporation may be amended by a vote of members who own 51% of the common elements. A certified copy of each by-law must be registered on the title in order for the by-law to be effective.

4. Rules and regulations

The rules and regulations of a condominium project are intended to govern the everyday rights and obligations of the unit owners. These rules and regulations are usually similar to the rules and regulations in force in a rental apartment building.

5. The condominium corporation

When a project is constituted as a condominium project, a corporation without share capital is created and the members of this corporation are the owners of the various units.

The Condominium Act also provides that the members of the corporation share the assets of the corporation in the same proportions as the proportions of their common interests, as set forth in the declaration. The objects of the condominium corporation are to manage the property and any assets of the corporation.

The condominium corporation is similar in operation to any other type of corporation and, of course, has a board of directors, requirements for meetings, officers and the keeping of corporate records. The members of the condominium corporation, being the unit owners, elect the directors and are eligible for election to the board of directors. However, it is not necessary in all condominiums that the eligible directors be unit owners.

As previously mentioned, the unit owners are eligible to vote at meetings of the condominium corporation. However, the Condominium Act provides that a mortgage of a unit may contain a provision authorizing the mortgagee (lender) to exercise the right of the unit owner to vote or to consent. If the mortgage contains such a provision, the mortgagee may, of course, exercise this right to vote or consent in place of the owner. The mortgagee will usually exercise this right to vote only in matters of great importance.

c. THINGS YOU SHOULD KNOW BEFORE BUYING

The first matter you should consider as a prospective buyer of a condominium is the location of the boundaries of the dwelling unit. These boundaries are established in the declaration and description that is registered on the title to the project when the project is constituted as a condominium and this determination is usually made by the builder, in conjunction with the lending institution that provides the mortgage financing for all of the units. It is important to determine the unit boundaries because from this you will know what portions of the condominium project are yours alone and what portions of the condominium project are to be shared with the other owners.

For example, in a row housing type of condominium project, each row house may have attached to it a patio, a backyard and a garage. If you, as a condominium unit owner, are the exclusive owner of your patio, backyard and garage, you have a legal right to require that other people do not interfere with your enjoyment of these amenities. However, if these items are common elements, your right to the enjoyment of these items is no greater than the right of any other unit owner in the condominium project, unless, of course, these items are described in the declaration as being limited common elements (common elements designated as being for the exclusive use of one unit owner).

As a further example, if the unit boundaries are the inside surface of the plaster walls, you will theoretically not be able to interfere with the plaster surface either by hanging a picture or by covering the plaster with panelling without interfering with the rights of all of the other unit owners. However, if the unit boundary is the outer surface of the plaster wall or the centre line of the structural wall, you will be free to hang pictures or whatever on the plaster because it is your plaster alone and not the plaster of all of the unit owners in the project.

In most condominium projects, the unit boundaries are usually established to provide that each of the unit owners will have control over the plaster surface of their unit and the condominium corporation will have control over the major structural items, including the water pipes, heating ducts and electrical wiring and other apparatus passing between the units. The purpose here is that, if any repairs are required to these items, the cost of the repairs will be absorbed by the entire ownership of the project rather than by a specific unit owner because these items service more than one unit owner.

The expenses of the condominium corporation are paid by all of the unit owners, usually on a monthly basis and these payments are known as common expenses. The ratio in which the total amount of the common expenses are apportioned among the units is set out in the declaration and, of course, the total of the percentages of all unit owners' common expenses will equal 100%.

By applying these ratios to the total amount required by the condominium corporation to be expended for the upkeep of the property and the satisfaction of all of the obligations of the condominium corporation, you can determine the amount of common expenses that are payable by each unit owner.

The Condominium Act recognizes the importance to all unit owners of the prompt payment of common expenses by all of the other unit owners and, accordingly, has provided that a lien may be claimed against individual titles to a condominium unit for the failure to pay common expenses. Further, this lien may be enforced in the same manner as the enforcement of a mortgage in default. The lien for common expenses is given priority over mortgages by the Condominium Act.

The Condominium Act also provides that certain restrictions may be set out in the declaration restricting an owner's rights to sell, lease or otherwise dispose of his or her unit. The reasoning behind such a provision is to make sure that the condominium project will not lose the character or identity that it originally was endowed with by the sale, lease or gift of a particular unit to someone who is considered undesirable.

Since a condominium declaration must be registered prior to any of the unit owners receiving their title to their unit, this character or quality must be in the project at a very early date.

In addition, it must be remembered that the declaration may be amended only with the consent of all unit owners and all persons having registered encumbrances against the units and common interest, such as mortgagees. Thus, it is difficult to change the character of a condominium project after it has been originally constituted.

If you are considering the purchase of a condominium unit, a prime concern will be the nature and extent of the restrictions on selling, leasing or giving of a unit prior to submitting an offer to purchase. Future plans must be considered regarding family planning, etc., and the type of condominium fitted in with these plans.

As previously mentioned, the keeping of a pet in a condominium project may be prohibited or restricted. Many people place great importance on their pets and, accordingly, you should make the appropriate inquiry prior to signing an offer to purchase.

Probably the greatest problem associated with current condominium conveyancing is the problem relating to a situation where occupancy is given to the purchaser some time, usually several months, before the purchaser receives title. This problem arises out of the fact that the Condominium Act requires that construction of the condominium project be substantially completed in accordance with the structural plans before the description can be registered and it is only when the description is registered that a project becomes governed by the act. Thus, in many projects the earliest units constructed are available for occupancy some time before the final units are constructed and the purchasers of these early units may wish to occupy them, despite the fact that title cannot be obtained until the project is registered as a condominium project.

Because most builders require that the purchaser pay the entire balance due on closing at the time of taking possession, you would be risking your money until you receive title. Thus, if the developer of the condominium project should become bankrupt before title can be given, you may lose the entire amount of your balance due on closing.

Recent amendments to the Condominium Act have reduced the risk for purchasers by requiring that developers hold this money in a trust account or insured type of arrangement. This recent amendment will certainly reduce the risk involved in buying a condominium unit. However, two problems remain — first, if the developer is dishonest, the purchaser may not be protected and, second, since the developer cannot use this money for that time, the purchase price will probably be increased. The legislation also provides for the developer to pay interest on trust monies. This will also bring a price increase.

A common advertising and marketing feature of modern condominiums is the "repurchase guarantee." The repurchase guarantee is not limited to the condominium market but has been most prevalent in this area.

It is an agreement between the unit owner and the builder or seller of the condominium units where the seller guarantees that the unit can be sold at a certain price and upon certain other terms and conditions. Failing this, the builder or seller agrees to repurchase the unit again on certain terms and conditions. These terms and conditions are important and should be carefully read. Such things as the amount at which the unit will be repurchased, any deductions from this purchase price, the time at which or during which the unit must be repurchased, the period of notice, if any, required to be given in order to exercise the repurchase guarantee and any other obligations upon the unit buyer in order to exercise the guarantee are all important.

Of course, the repurchase guarantee and all of its workings should be set forth in the offer or in a schedule to the offer.

Since the lending institution providing the mortgage money usually has the largest financial interest in the condominium project, they will often require the builder of the condominium to undertake the management of the project for a specified period of time, usually two to five years. In this way, the lending institution attempts to provide a manager for the unit owners who has intimate knowledge of the workings of the project and, in addition, attempts to encourage the developer to establish a workable, reasonable and efficient condominium government.

Thus, it is usual to find that the condominium corporation has entered into a management agreement with a manager who undertakes to fulfill all of the obligations of the condominium corporation with respect to the management and operation of the property and, of course, the manager will usually receive a fee for these services. You should read the management agreement to become familiar with all of the rights and duties of the manager.

The Condominium Act permits unit owners to terminate any management agreement entered into at a time when the developer was the owner of substantially all of the units. This termination can only occur if the owners pass the appropriate by-law with a 51% vote, and if they give 60 days' notice.

An agreement of purchase and sale for a new condominium unit being purchased from the condominium developer is not binding on the purchaser until the current disclosure statement and all its material amendments have been delivered to the purchaser. The purchaser, before receiving title to his or her unit, may rescind the agreement of purchase and sale within 10 days after receiving the disclosure statement or a material amendment of the disclosure statement. This is known as the "cooling off" period. Upon rescission, the purchaser is entitled to receive a refund of the purchase price. The disclosure statement must contain:

(a) The name and address of the developer and of the project

(b) A general description of the project, including the types and number of buildings, units and recreational or other amenities together with any conditions that apply to the provision of amenities

(c) The portion of units which the developer intends to market in blocks of units to investors

(d) A brief narrative description of the significant

features of the declaration, by-laws and rules governing the use of common elements and units and of any contracts or leases that may be subject to termination after one year, unless ratified by the board of directors elected after the developer ceases to own one-half of the units

(e) A budget statement for one year after the registration of the declaration creating the condominium. This budget statement is warranted by the developer. In other words, in most circumstances, the developer will be required to make up any deficiencies in this budget statement if there is a shortfall

(f) Where construction of amenities is not completed, a schedule of the proposed beginning and completion dates

The budget statement mentioned in item (e) must include:

(a) The common expenses

(b) The proposed amount of each expense

(c) Particulars of the type, frequency and level of the services to be provided

(d) The projected monthly common expense contribution for each type of unit

(e) A statement of the portion of the common expense to be paid into the reserve fund

(f) A statement of the assumed inflation factor

(g) A statement of any judgments against the corporation, the status of any pending lawsuits to which the corporation is a party and the status of any pending lawsuits material to the project of which the developer has actual knowledge

(h) Any current or expected fees or charges to be paid by unit owners or any of them for the use of the common elements or part of them and other facilities related to the property

(i) Any services or expenses not included in the budget that the developer provided or paid for that might reasonably be expected to become, at any subsequent time, a common expense, and the projected common expense contribution attributable to each of those services or expenses for each type of unit

(j) The amounts in all reserve funds

d. COMMON EXPENSES

Each owner is required to contribute to the cost of maintaining the common facilities and obligations of the condominium corporation. This is called the common expenses and may include the following.

(a) Gardening in the common areas or, perhaps, at all of the units

(b) Snow removal

(c) Salary and supply of accommodation for a superintendent, caretaker or doorman

(d) Salary of a lifeguard and maintenance of the swimming pool

(e) Supply and upkeep of common recreational facilities, such as ping pong tables

(f) Premiums for the insurance policies maintained by the condominium corporation

(g) Fees paid to the project manager

The amount of the common expenses is determined by multiplying the cost of the common expenses by the percentage contained in the declaration as the percentage contribution to the common expenses.

The cost of the common expenses is usually estimated in advance and this amount is usually required to be paid on a monthly basis. An example of this is as follows:

The board of directors of the condominium corporation estimates that the total cost for common facilities, etc., for 1985 will be $360 000. Your percentage contribution to the common expenses is .06%. Therefore, during 1985 your common expenses will be $216 and your declaration and by-laws require you to pay this in monthly instalments of $18.

Common expenses are subject to increase or decrease. In the above example, if the board of directors estimate the 1985 costs will be $360 000, 1985 monthly payments will be $18. Similarly, if 1985 costs end up to be $400 000 rather than the estimated $360 000, our unit owner will have to pay an additional $24 during 1986.

Common expenses may also be increased by making additions, alterations or improvements to the common elements. The Condominium Act allows the members of the condominium corporation to vote on whether an addition, alteration or improvement is substantial. However, if the vote is carried, the cost of the addition, alteration or improvement becomes a common expense.

If a unit owner does not pay his or her common expenses, the condominium corporation obtains a lien against the title of that unit owner. This lien is an enforceable claim against the real estate and, of course, the unit owner will have great difficulty in selling his or her unit unless the lien is removed from the title. This lien may be enforced in the same manner as a mortgage (i.e., by foreclosure and sale of the unit).

If one of your neighbors does not pay his or her common expenses, you may have the condominium corporation pursue its remedies because each unit owner is entitled to have the other unit owners comply with the Condominium Act, the declaration and the by-laws. Thus, only when all remedies have failed to prove successful will a unit owner be required to absorb the default of another unit owner in failing to pay common expenses.

e. INSURANCE REQUIREMENTS IN A CONDOMINIUM

Insurance is an extremely important aspect of any purchase of real property and this is particularly true in a condominium project because of the community type of living and inter-dependence of unit owners.

Insurance in a condominium project is a complex matter and, rather than going into this topic in great detail, we shall briefly describe the various types of insurance required by the condominium purchaser. Your lawyer will advise you as to your basic coverage requirements; however, we strongly suggest that you contact your own insurance agent who will assist you in obtaining all of the coverage that you require.

1. Fire and extended perils coverage

This type of insurance coverage protects against destruction of the *structural* portion of the home by fire and other similar dangers. The condominium corporation is now required to obtain this coverage for the units and the common elements.

Because of the nature of condominiums, the amount of this type of insurance coverage should be sufficient, in total, to replace the entire amount of the project that may be destroyed. It is in the interest of all unit owners to make sure that the insurance company will pay for the replacement of the unit.

2. Improvements

If the fire insurance coverage is obtained by the condominium corporation, it is most likely that the coverage will not extend to the improvements you make, such as built-in shelving units, extra cabinets or wall panelling. If you make improvements to the unit, you should have them insured yourself.

3. Contents

The insurance policy obtained by the condominium corporation will probably not cover the risk of loss or damage to the contents of the condominium unit. You should obtain protection for your own contents, such as furniture, appliances, furs, cameras, broadloom, etc.

4. Liability

This type of coverage is to protect against personal injury or damage to property of people who are not unit owners. For example, if a guest of one of the unit owners falls on a patch of ice that should have been cleared, that person may have a claim against the condominium corporation or the unit owner or both. The condominium corporation will

74

probably carry this type of insurance but, *in addition*, each unit owner should also obtain sufficient liability insurance protection.

5. Conclusion

After reading the above, you can see that three points become important in insuring your condominium unit.

(a) Because the condominium corporation has obtained insurance coverage, you are not relieved of your obligation (to yourself) to make sure that the coverage is adequate with respect to both the type and the amount of coverage.

(b) Your lawyer will offer some assistance in arranging your insurance protection but, ultimately, this is something you should do with your insurance agent, who has the experience in this complex area and who can better advise you as to your individual requirements.

(c) Don't hesitate to spend a few extra dollars to get full coverage for all of your needs. Too many people have suffered severe financial hardships from a fire or other accident because they were under-insured.

5

RULES REGARDING NON-RESIDENTS

a. ARE YOU PURCHASING PROPERTY FROM A NON-RESIDENT?

Section 116 of the Income Tax Act deals with the purchase of any property from people who are not residents of Canada within the meaning of the Income Tax Act.

A person who is not a resident of Canada is subject to a tax of 15% on capital gains obtained in Canada. The problem of imposing a tax on non-residents of Canada is the collection of the tax; section 116 of the Income Tax Act attempts to enforce collection of the tax from the vendor by putting a very large responsibility on the purchaser of property.

Under this section, a vendor who is not a resident of Canada is required to apply to the government of Canada for a certificate which, when issued, will set a maximum price that a purchaser may pay for the property of the non-resident without being liable for any payment to the government of Canada.

Thus, if the purchaser pays a greater price than that set forth in the certificate, the purchaser may be responsible for tax on the difference between the price paid and the certificate limit.

The Income Tax Act further imposes a responsibility on the purchaser to make reasonable inquiries to determine the country of residence of the vendor. If the purchaser fails to make these inquiries, the act provides that the *purchaser* will be responsible for the payment of the 15% tax.

It is the general opinion that in cases where a non-resident vendor does not apply for the certificate and the purchaser nevertheless completes the transaction, the purchaser will be responsible for 15% of the entire purchase price, the certificate limit in this instance being zero. Thus, it is common in current real estate transactions for the purchaser to require from the vendor either the certificate described in section 116 of the act or evidence usually in the form of a sworn statement from the vendor that he or she is a resident of Canada within the meaning of section 116.

What happens if the vendor is unwilling to apply for the necessary certificate or if the vendor is unwilling to provide satisfactory evidence of residency in Canada and the purchaser chooses to sign the agreement anyway? It creates a real dilemma, since it is felt that the provisions of section 116 of the act do not amount to a lien against the real estate but remain as personal obligations between the parties.

Thus, if the vendor should fail to comply with his or her responsibilities under section 116 the purchaser cannot refuse to complete the transaction on the basis that the vendor is not conveying a good title. If the purchaser refuses to close, he or she may be liable to the vendor for the loss of the deposit, specific performance or damages. On the other hand, if the purchaser completes the transaction, he or she may be liable to the government of Canada for 15% of the entire purchase price.

This problem has been avoided in recent versions of many standard agreement of purchase and sale forms by placing an obligation on the vendor to comply with the requirements of section 116 either by obtaining the requisite certificate or, alternatively, by providing satisfactory evidence of residency in Canada. However, this problem exists if the standard form is not used or if the form that is used does not contain the appropriate clauses.

It is important to keep in mind that the term "residency" has a specific meaning for the purposes of the Income Tax Act and this term also applies to corporations, associations of people and trusts and, thus, the purchase of real estate from a company or a firm or an estate does not relieve the purchaser of obligations under this section.

b. ARE YOU A NON-RESIDENT PURCHASING PROPERTY IN ONTARIO?

The Land Transfer Act of Ontario distinguishes between a "resident" purchaser and a "non-resident" purchaser, the difference leading to a substantial difference in amount of tax payable (see chapter 9). Non-residents pay much more tax.

The Land Transfer Tax Act permits a non-resident purchaser to pay the "resident" rate of land transfer tax if the non-resident purchaser is purchasing "unrestricted land." "Unrestricted land" is defined as land that is *assessed* by the municipality for use for residential, commercial or industrial uses.

However, two problems usually relate to the purchase by a non-resident of a home in Ontario. First, in many situations, the non-resident purchaser is not aware of the differential in rate of land transfer tax payable by the non-resident purchaser. Again, we suggest contacting an adviser before submitting an offer to purchase.

Second, there is usually not sufficient time between finding the home and making the offer to obtain confirmation that lands are *assessed* in such a way that will qualify as "unrestricted land." We suggest that a clause be added to the offer to purchase by the non-resident purchaser obligating the vendor to have the transfer or deed stamped as being "unrestricted land" prior to delivery to the purchaser on closing or at least giving the purchaser's adviser some specified period of time (during which the agreement can be made conditional) to obtain the necessary confirmation.

6

FINANCING YOUR HOME

a. INTRODUCTION

If you purchase a new home, whether it be a fully detached or semi-detached house, condominium or co-op unit, you will almost invariably be required to deal through a mortgage institution dictated by the builder. In this case, you may refer directly to the section on mortgage financing (see page 81) for a complete discussion of mortgages.

If you are purchasing an older home, you will have a greater choice of financing methods and the method selected will depend almost entirely on your negotiations with the vendor. Where possible, the easiest and simplest method of financing is to have the purchaser carry the balance or assume the vendor's mortgage. The pros and cons of the various types of financing are discussed below.

b. THE OLDER HOME

There are three common ways you can arrange mortgage financing on the purchase of an older home.

 (a) You assume the vendor's existing mortgage.
 (b) You arrange your own mortgage financing and, accordingly, the vendor discharges his or her previous mortgage financing.
 (c) The purchaser gives you back a mortgage.

These methods of arranging mortgage financing are not mutually exclusive and, in fact, many real estate transactions are completed on the basis of a combination of these types of financing.

If you assume the vendor's existing mortgage, you are, in effect, assuming the remainder of the vendor's obligations to the mortgagee (lender) under a mortgage contract that was arranged some time prior to your entering into this agreement. In this situation, you are usually not able to negotiate any of the terms of the mortgage because they have already been established. You merely take over the obligations of the vendor under the mortgage in accordance with its terms.

In periods of rising interest rates, it may be advantageous to assume the vendor's mortgage if the interest rate is lower than the rate currently available.

When you and the vendor agree that the vendor will take back a mortgage for a portion of the purchase price, you must negotiate the terms of this mortgage in the same way that you negotiate every other term of the offer to purchase. In fact, the negotiation of the mortgage back will be included in the offer and, accordingly, will be a part of the negotiation for the purchase of the house. Thus, in your offer you must specify the amount of the mortgage to be taken by the vendor, the interest rate, the terms of repayment, the length of period for which the mortgage will run and any privileges for prepayment or renewal.

If you are not satisfied with the vendor's existing mortgage or with the terms of the mortgage that the vendor is willing to take back, you must try to make your financing arrangements with someone else, usually a bank or a trust company. In this case you would put in the offer that the deal is conditional upon your being able to arrange mortgage financing within certain limits. Thus, you should submit a conditional offer to purchase; conditional upon you arranging a mortgage for a minimum amount for a minimum term at a maximum interest rate with a maximum repayment amount.

On the other side, a vendor may not wish to accept an agreement of purchase and sale that is conditional because during the time in which you are attempting to arrange this mortgage financing, he or she will not be able to sell the home if another offer should be submitted.

In other words, the prudent vendor will usually not be willing to accept an offer to purchase that is conditional upon any matters that are not within his or her control.

However, if the vendor does accept such an offer, you are then under an obligation to search all the avenues that are available in order to obtain the requisite mortgage financing.

In many situations, you may only be able to obtain mortgage financing that is less favorable than the limits set out in the offer. In this case, it may be up to you to waive the condition in the offer and complete the transaction anyway, if you wish.

c. ALL ABOUT MORTGAGES
1. Introduction
Many people understand that a mortgage is a loan of money repayable with interest and that the mortgage is given on the security of real estate. Normally this is the extent of their understanding of the situation and it is the purpose of this section to briefly discuss the workings and practical aspects of mortgages.

A mortgage, as it is called in the Registry Act system, is properly called a charge if the land is registered under the Land Titles Act system. The reason for the designation of the mortgage as a charge is that a mortgage charges or pledges certain land as security for the payment of certain monies and the performance of certain obligations. Until recently, a mortgage and a charge were different forms with similar content. However, since 1984, the same form (now called a "Charge/Mortgage of Land" — see Sample Form #4) is used, regardless of whether the land is recorded under the Land Titles Act system or the Registry Act system. For the purposes of this book, a mortgage and a charge are both referred to as a mortgage.

2. What is a mortgage?
A mortgage is a loan of money from a money lender (mortgagee) to an owner of land (mortgagor) whereby the mortgagor provides as security for the loan of money a conveyance of an interest in the land to the mortgagee. In fact, a mortgage is a conveyance by the mortgagor to the

mortgagee of all of the mortgagor's interest in the land, except the following:

(a) The mortgagor's right of possession

(b) The mortgagor's right to redeem the mortgaged property from the mortgagee upon payment of the mortgage account

In other words, when a mortgage is given, the mortgagee becomes the legal owner of the property, subject to the right of the mortgagor to have possession of the premises and subject to the further right of the mortgagor to obtain reconveyance of the property upon payment of the mortgage account.

Thus, it may be seen that a mortgage is more than a loan of money — it is an actual conveyance of the property subject to the retention of certain rights by the mortgagor. In addition, the mortgagor makes several covenants in the mortgage document that require the fulfillment of various obligations during the term of the mortgage. Some of these obligations are discussed later in this section.

3. Types of mortgages

There are basically two types of mortgages, differing in the manner of repayment.

One type of mortgage may require the mortgagor to repay specific amounts of principal on each payment date plus interest on the outstanding principal over the instalment period. For example, the mortgagor may be required to pay $100 on account of principal plus interest quarterly. In this type of mortgage, the principal portion of each payment remains the same and the interest portion is reduced for each successive payment. Thus, in this type of mortgage, each payment is less than the last one.

The second type of mortgage is commonly called an amortized mortgage and in this mortgage, each payment is of equal amount. Each equal payment is divided into principal and interest in different proportions over the life of the mortgage. For example, if an amortized mortgage is repayable in monthly instalments of $250 each, the first payment may consist of $235 in interest and $15 in principal and the last payment under this mortgage may consist of $20 of interest and $230 of principal.

The type of mortgage in each particular circumstance is a matter of negotiation between the mortgagee and the mortgagor. Most institutional lenders of money will insist upon using an amortized type of mortgage arrangement.

4. Term and amortization period

Many people find these terms confusing, and feel that, because payments extend over, for example, 20 years then the term of the mortgage is 20 years. The word "term," however, refers to the length of time that the mortgagee will lend the money to the mortgagor. At the end of the term, the mortgagor is required to repay the balance owing to the mortgagee. In most cases the term is shorter than the amortization period. The usual term in the current mortgage market is five years. Thus, if a $12 000 mortgage, repayable in monthly instalments of $100 on account of principal, is for a five-year term, the mortgagor will be required to repay to the mortgagee the sum of $6 000 at the end of the five-year term.

The phrase "amortization period" means the length of time that it would take for the mortgage to be paid in full if all of the instalments were to be made. Thus, a mortgage of $12 000, repayable in monthly principal payments of $100, would be fully amortized over a period of 10 years because at the end of the 10 year period, there would be no balance to be paid under the mortgage by the mortgagor.

It is quite common for the term of the mortgage to be a different length of time (that is shorter length of time) than the amortization period. In fact, this is a common occurrence in the present mortgage market, where a mortgage may be available for a five-year term and a 25-year amortization period. In this situation, the mortgagor at the end of the five-year term is required to pay a substantial amount to the mortgagee in payment of the mortgagee's account. If the mortgagor does not have the funds available at the end of the term, arrangements will have to be made to refinance the outstanding balance, either with the same lender or with a new lender.

5. Use of standard forms

Sample #4 is the form of a charge/mortgage of land that may be used under either the Registry Act system or the Land Titles Act system. The only difference is the description of the land which is contained in box 5 of the form. This form considers the payment of a consistent amount of principal and varying amounts of interest, resulting in a variable monthly payment that decreases over the lifespan of the mortgage. In order to transform this mortgage into an amortized mortgage plan (i.e., variable amounts of principal and interest but a consistent monthly payment), boxes 9(e) and 9(h) would be completed differently.

In addition to the mortgage document, such as Sample #4, a charge/mortgage of land will usually have additional terms that are incorporated into the transaction by referring to standard charge terms, such as those shown in Sample #5. These standard charge terms can be incorporated by referring to their number in the Land Registry Office (as is shown in box 8 of Sample #4) or they can be made a schedule to the charge/mortgage of land. Anyone can file standard charge terms with the Land Registry Office and many of the institutional lenders have done so. Once filed, the terms can be incorporated into the charge/mortgage of land by reference to their filing number, instead of having to be attached as a schedule.

Although it is not clearly stated in the charge/mortgage of land document or in the standard charge terms used by most lenders, it is important to realize that the person who originally signed the mortgage is liable under the mortgage even if the home is sold. If Ms. Ursula Unwary sells her home to Walter Welsher and he doesn't pay the mortgage instalments under the mortgage originally given by Ursula to Martin Mortgagee and assumed by Walter, Ursula will find that she is still liable and Martin Mortgagee may proceed against her for the amount. Ms. Unwary may take action against Walter Welsher and is entitled to receive an assignment of the mortgage from Martin Mortgagee upon her paying what is owing under it. However, in these circumstances, it is often the case that the property is not as valuable as the amount owing under the mortgage.

SAMPLE #4
CHARGE/MORTGAGE OF LAND

Province of Ontario	**Charge/Mortgage of Land** Form 2 — Land Registration Reform Act, 1984		**B**

(1) Registry [X]   **Land Titles** [ ]   **(2)** Page 1 of 1 pages

(3) Property Identifier(s)   Block   Property   Additional: See Schedule [ ]

(4) Principal Amount

Six Thousand Two Hundred......... Dollars $ 6,200.00

(5) Description

Lot 62, Plan 10572, City of Toronto,
Municipality of Metropolitan Toronto

New Property Identifiers   Additional: See Schedule [ ]

Executions   Additional: See Schedule [ ]

(6) This Document Contains (a) Redescription New Easement Plan/Sketch [ ] (b) Schedule for: Additional Description [ ] Parties [ ] Other [ ]   **(7) Interest/Estate Charged** Fee Simple

(8) Standard Charge Terms — The parties agree to be bound by the provisions in Standard Charge Terms filed as number 851 and the Chargor(s) hereby acknowledge(s) receipt of a copy of these terms.

(9) Payment Provisions

(a) Principal Amount $ 6,200.00   (b) Interest Rate 8¼ % per annum   (c) Calculation Period quarter-yearly

(d) Interest Adjustment Date 1985 06 30   (e) Payment Date and Period Quarter-yearly on last days of March, June, September and December   (f) First Payment Date 1985 09 30

(g) Last Payment Date 1990 03 31   (h) Amount of Each Payment One Hundred Dollars ($100.00) on account of principal plus interest on the unpaid balance ~~Dollars $~~

(i) Balance Due Date 1990 06 30   (i) Insurance FULL REPLACEMENT VALUE   Dollars $

(10) Additional Provisions The Mortgagors, when not in default, may prepay the whole or any part of the principal sum hereby secured without notice or bonus.
The Mortgagors, when not in default, may renew the within Charge/Mortgage for a further term of 4 years upon the same terms and conditions, save as to the right of further renewal.   Continued on Schedule [ ]

(11) Chargor(s) The chargor hereby charges the land to the charges and certifies that the chargor is at least eighteen years old and that

...... we. are. spouses .of. one .another.......

The chargor(s) acknowledge(s) receipt of a true copy of this charge.

Name(s)	Signature(s)	Date of Signature Y M D
PURCHASER, Peter	*Peter Purchaser*	1985 06 23
PURCHASER, Paula	*Paula Purchaser*	1985 06 23

(12) Spouse(s) of Chargor(s) I hereby consent to this transaction.
Name(s)   Signature(s)   Date of Signature Y M D

(13) Chargor(s) Address for Service

123 Any Street, Toronto, Ontario, M1N 2O3

(14) Chargee(s)

VENDOR, Violet

(15) Chargee(s) Address for Service

456 Some Street, Toronto, Ontario, M7Q 8R9

(16) Assessment Roll Number of Property Cty 06 Mun. 35 Map 060 Sub 000 Par 00000   Fees   Registration Fee

(17) Municipal Address of Property

123 Any Street
Toronto, Ontario

(18) Document Prepared by:

I. M. RIGHT
Barrister and Solicitor
56 Chancery Lane
Toronto, Ontario
M4L 5N6

Total

10172 (12/84)

Charge/Mortgage of Land

IMPORTANT NOTICE

I.   It is a serious offence under the Criminal Code to make a false statement in this document.

II. This document should be registered in the proper Land Registry Office.

III. When registered, this document is the property of the Land Registry Office.

INSTRUCTIONS FOR COMPLETION

(1) Registry/Land Titles — Mark "x" in the appropriate box.

(2) Pages — Enter total number of pages of document, including this form.

(3) Property Identifier(s) — If identifier(s) has/have been assigned by the Land Registry Office, insert a maximum of two here. If land charged has more than two identifiers enter two here and mark the "Additional See Schedule" box with an "x" and attach schedule with remaining identifier(s).

(4) Principal Amount — Enter total amount to be secured by the charge, whether actually advanced or not, first in words then in numbers. Do not use "$2.00 and other consideration." In Land Titles, a monetary amount must be shown (e.g. not to exceed $100,000.00). In Registry, if the principal amount cannot be set out conveniently in this box, enter "See Schedule".

(5) Description — Begin with parcel and section (Land Titles), part, lot or unit on plan or concession lot (e.g. Unit 13, Level 13, York Condominium Plan No. 25 or Part Lot 6, Concession 6). Include also the township, municipality, etc. If a metes and bounds description is required, mark "x" in box 6(b) and attach schedule with full description. For condominium properties, enter a reference to the Land Registry Office in which the plan is registered.

(6) This Document Contains — Mark either box (a) or (b) with an "x" as required.

(7) Interest/Estate Charged — Add qualifier if required. Delete fee simple if not applicable and enter the interest/estate charged (e.g. leasehold [Land Titles], life estate, etc.).

(8) Standard Charge Terms — Enter filing number for the set of standard charge terms.

(9) Payment Provisions — If the payment provisions cannot be entered conveniently in the format provided, mark box 6(b) with an "x" and attach a schedule. Box (a) Enter in numbers only. (b) Enter interest rate. (c) Enter interest calculation period and dates if necessary (e.g. quarterly, semi-annually, March 15th and September 15th etc.). (d) Enter interest adjustment date. (e) Enter date and period of each payment (e.g. 15th monthly). (f) Enter first regular payment date. (g) Enter last regular payment date. (h) Enter amount in both words and numbers. (i) Enter date on which balance owing under charge is due. (j) Enter amount in both words and numbers OR state "See Standard Charge Terms No. (insert no.)" OR "See Schedule" if the amount cannot be set out conveniently here. If no insurance is required, enter "Not Required". In Land Titles, for an instrument in the nature of a deed of trust and mortgage that provides for the issuance of bonds or debentures, set out the aggregate principal sum and interest rate in 9(a) and 9(b).

(10) Additional Provisions — Enter here (e.g. Pre-payment privileges, Interest Act). If space is insufficient check the "Continued on Schedule" box and box 6(b) with an "x" and attach a schedule.

(11) Chargor(s) — For natural persons, at least one of the following statements regarding compliance with the Family Law Reform Act must be entered: (1) We are spouses of one another. (2) The person consenting below is my spouse. (3) I am not a spouse. (4) The property charged has never been occupied by me and my spouse as our matrimonial home. (5) The property is not designated under section 41 of the Family Law Reform Act and there is an instrument designating another property as our matrimonial home which has been registered and has not been cancelled. (6) My spouse has released all rights under Part III of the Family Law Reform Act by a separation agreement. (7) This transaction is authorized by court order under section 44 of the Family Law Reform Act registered as instrument no. (insert no.) which has not been stayed. (8) A court order has been made releasing the property as a matrimonial home registered as instrument no. (insert no.) which has not been stayed.

In Land Titles, for natural persons enter the names of the chargors as they appear in the parcel register with the last name first in capitals. In Registry, for natural persons enter the last name first in capitals. Where possible, enter each chargor on a separate line. For corporate chargors, enter the entire name in capitals as well as the name of the person authorized to sign on behalf of the corporation. If the corporation has not used a seal, add "I/We have authority to bind the corporation."

The capacity and share for each chargor may be stated. Express share as a percentage or a fraction. Mark box 6(b) with an "x" and attach a schedule if more space is required.

(12) Spouse(s) of Chargor(s) — Enter last name(s) of each/all consenting spouse(s) on separate lines in capitals followed by the first and middle name(s).

(13) Chargor(s) Address for Service — Enter full address including postal code.

(14) Chargee(s) — For natural persons, enter last name first in capitals, followed by the first and at least one middle name. Where possible, enter each chargee on a separate line. The capacity and share for each chargee may be stated here. Express share as a percentage or a fraction. Mark box 6(b) with an "x" and attach a schedule if more space is required. For corporate chargees, enter the entire name in capitals.

(15) Chargee(s) Address for Service — Enter full address including postal code.

(16) Assessment Roll Number of Property — If assigned, enter here. If not assigned by the municipality, enter "NOT ASSIGNED". If property charged has more than one assessment roll number, enter "MULTIPLE". Information entered does NOT affect the validity of this document.

(17) Municipal Address of Property — Enter full municipal address of property. State as follows: street number, suffix (e.g. "A" as in 29A), street name, unit type (apt., suite etc.), unit number, municipality, postal code. If property charged has more than one municipal address, enter "MULTIPLE". Information entered does NOT affect the validity of this document.

(18) Document Prepared by — Enter name and address including postal code.

FOR OFFICE USE ONLY		
This document has been		Duplicate for
Registered/Received ____	Verified/Certified ____	Name and Address
Abstracted ____	Filmed ____	

SAMPLE #5
STANDARD CHARGE TERMS

Land Registration Reform Act, 1984

SET OF STANDARD CHARGE TERMS

Filed by

Filing Date:

Filing number:

The following Set of Standard Charge Terms shall be deemed to be included in every charge in which the set is referred to by its filing number, as provided in section 9 of the Act.

Exclusion of Statutory Covenants

1. The implied covenants deemed to be included in a charge under sub-section 7(1) of the Land Registration Reform Act, 1984, and shown as paragraphs 1 and 2 of the said sub-section 7(1), shall be and are hereby expressly excluded and replaced by this Set of Standard Charge Terms which are covenants by the Chargor, for the Chargor and the Chargor's successors, with the Chargee and the Chargee's successors and assigns.

Right to Charge the Land

2. The Chargor now has good right, full power and lawful and absolute authority to charge the land and to give the Charge to the Chargee upon the covenants contained in the Charge.

No Act to Encumber

3. The Chargor has not done, committed, executed or wilfully or knowingly suffered any act, deed, matter or thing whatsoever whereby or by means whereof the land, or any part or parcel thereof, is or shall or may be in any way impeached, charged, affected or encumbered in title, estate or otherwise, except as the records of the land registry office disclose.

Good Title in Fee Simple

4. The Chargor, at the time of the execution and delivery of the Charge, is, and stands solely, rightfully and lawfully seized of a good, sure, perfect, absolute and indefeasible estate of inheritance, in fee simple, of and in the land and the premises described in the Charge and in every part and parcel thereof without any manner of trusts, reservations, limitations, provisos, conditions or any other matter or thing to alter, charge, change, encumber or defeat the same, except those contained in the original grant thereof from the Crown.

Promise to Pay and Perform

5. The Chargor will pay or cause to be paid to the Chargee the full principal amount and interest secured by the Charge in the manner of payment provided by the Charge, without any deduction or abatement, and shall do, observe, perform, fulfill and keep all the provisions, covenants, agreements and stipulations contained in the Charge and shall pay as they fall due all taxes, rates and assessments, municipal, local, parliamentary and otherwise which now are or may hereafter be imposed, charged or levied upon the land and when required shall produce for the Chargee receipts evidencing payment of the same.

Interest After Default

6. In case default shall be made in payment of any sum to become due for interest at the time provided for payment in the Charge, compound interest shall be payable and the sum in arrears for interest from time to time, as well after as before maturity, shall bear interest at the rate provided for in the Charge. In case the interest and compound interest are not paid within the interest calculation period provided in the Charge from the time of default a rest shall be made, and compound interest at the rate provided for in the Charge shall be payable on the aggregate amount then due, as well after as before maturity, and so on from time to time, and all such interest and compound interest shall be a charge upon the land.

No Obligation to Advance

7. Neither the preparation, execution or registration of the Charge shall bind the Chargee to advance the principal amount secured, nor shall the advance of a part of the principal amount secured bind the Chargee to advance any unadvanced portion thereof, but nevertheless the security in the land shall take effect forthwith upon the execution of the Charge by the Chargor. The expenses of the examination of the title and of the Charge and valuation are to be secured by the Charge in the event of the whole or any balance of the principal amount not being advanced, the same to be charged hereby upon the land, and shall be without demand therefor, payable forthwith with interest at the rate provided for in the Charge, and in default the Chargee's power of sale hereby given, and all other remedies hereunder, shall be exercisable.

Costs Added to Principal

8. The Chargee may pay all premiums of insurance and all taxes, rates, levies, charges, assessments, utility and heating charges which shall from time to time fall due and be unpaid in respect of the land, and that such payments, together with all costs, charges, legal fees (as between solicitor and client) and expenses which may be incurred in taking, recovering and keeping possession of the land and of negotiating the Charge, investigating title, and registering the Charge and other necessary deeds, and generally in any other proceedings taken in connection with or to realize upon the security given in the Charge (including legal fees and real estate commissions and other costs incurred in leasing or selling the land or in exercising the power of entering, lease and sale contained in the Charge) shall be, with interest at the rate provided for in the Charge, a charge upon the land in favour of the Chargee pursuant to the terms of the Charge and the Chargee may pay or satisfy any lien, charge or encumbrance now existing or hereafter created or claimed upon the land, which payments with interest at the rate provided for in the Charge shall likewise be a charge upon the land in favour of the Chargee. Provided, and it is hereby further agreed, that all amounts paid by the Chargee as aforesaid shall be added to the principal amount secured by the Charge and shall be payable forthwith with interest at the rate provided for in the Charge, and on default all sums secured by the Charge shall immediately become due and payable at the option of the Chargee, and all powers in the Charge conferred shall become exercisable.

SAMPLE #5 — Continued

Power of Sale

9. The Chargee on default of payment for at least fifteen (15) days may, on at least thirty-five (35) days' notice in writing given to the Chargor, enter on and lease the land or sell the land. Such notice shall be given to such persons and in such manner and form and within such time as provided in the Mortgages Act. In the event that the giving of such notice shall not be required by law or to the extent that such requirements shall not be applicable, it is agreed that notice may be effectually given by leaving it with a grown-up person on the land, if occupied, or by placing it on the land if unoccupied, or at the option of the Chargee, by mailing it in a registered letter addressed to the Chargor at his last known address, or by publishing it once in a newspaper published in the county or district in which the land is situate, and such notice shall be sufficient although not addressed to any person or persons by name or designation; and notwithstanding that any person to be affected thereby may be unknown, unascertained, or under disability. Provided further, that in case default be made in the payment of the principal amount or interest or any part thereof and such default continues for two months after any payment of either falls due then the Chargee may exercise the foregoing powers of entering, leasing or selling or any of them without any notice, it being understood and agreed, however, that if the giving of notice by the Chargee shall be required by law then notice shall be given to such persons and in such manner and form and within such time as so required by law. It is hereby further agreed that the whole or any part or parts of the land may be sold by public auction or private contract, or partly one or partly the other; and that the proceeds of any sale hereunder may be applied first in payment of any costs, charges and expenses incurred in taking, recovering or keeping possession of the land or by reason of non-payment or procuring payment of monies, secured by the Charge or otherwise, and secondly in payment of all amounts of principal and interest owing under the Charge; and if any surplus shall remain after fully satisfying the claims of the Chargee as aforesaid same shall be paid to the Chargor or as he may direct. The Chargee may sell any of the land on such terms as to credit and otherwise as shall appear to him most advantageous and for such prices as can reasonably be obtained therefor and may make any stipulations as to title or evidence or commencement of title or otherwise which he shall deem proper, and may buy in or rescind or vary any contract for the sale of the whole or any part of the land and resell without being answerable for loss occasioned thereby, and in the case of a sale on credit the Chargee shall be bound to pay the Chargor only such monies as have been actually received from purchasers after the satisfaction of the claims of the Chargee and for any of said purposes may make and execute all agreements and assurances as he shall think fit. Any purchaser or lessee shall not be bound to see to the propriety or regularity of any sale or lease or be affected by express notice that any sale or lease is improper and no want of notice or publication when required hereby shall invalidate any sale or lease hereunder.

Quiet Possession

10. Where the Chargee enters on and takes possession of the land on default as described in paragraph 9 herein the Chargee shall enter into, have, hold, use, occupy, possess and enjoy the land without the let, suit, hindrance, interruption or denial of the Chargor or any other person or persons whomsoever.

Right to Distrain

11. If the Chargor shall make default in payment of any part of the interest payable under the Charge at any of the dates or times fixed for the payment thereof, it shall be lawful for the Chargee to distrain therefor upon the land or any part thereof, and by distress warrant, to recover by way of rent reserved, as in the case of a demise of the land, so much of such interest as shall, from time to time, be or remain in arrears and unpaid, together with all costs, charges and expenses attending such levy or distress, as in like cases of distress for rent. Provided that the Chargee may distrain for arrears of principal in the same manner as if the same were arrears of interest.

Further Assurances

12. From and after default in the payment of the principal amount secured by the Charge or the interest thereon or any part of such principal or interest or in the doing, observing, performing, fulfilling or keeping of some one or more of the covenants set forth in the Charge then and in every such case the Chargor and all and every other person whosoever having, or lawfully claiming, or who shall have or lawfully claim any estate, right, title, interest or trust of, in, to or out of the land shall, from time to time, at all times thereafter, at the proper costs and charges of the Chargor make, do, suffer and execute, or cause or procure to be made, done, suffered and executed, all and every such further and other reasonable act or acts, deed or deeds, devises, conveyances and assurances in the law for the further, better and more perfectly and absolutely conveying and assuring the land unto the Chargee as by the Chargee or his solicitor shall or may be lawfully and reasonably devised, advised or required.

Acceleration of Principal and Interest

13. In default of the payment of the interest secured by the Charge, the principal amount secured by the Charge shall, at the option of the Chargee, immediately become payable, and upon default of payment of instalments of principal promptly as the same mature, the balance of the principal and interest secured by the Charge shall, at the option of the Chargee, immediately become due and payable. The Chargee may in writing at any time or times after default waive such default and any such waiver shall apply only to the particular default waived and shall not operate as a waiver of any other or future default.

Partial Releases

14. The Chargee may at his discretion at all times release any part or parts of the land or any other security or any surety for the money secured under the Charge either with or without any sufficient consideration therefor, without responsibility therefor, and without thereby releasing any other part of the land or any person from the Charge or from any of the covenants contained in the Charge and without being accountable to the Chargor for the value thereof, or for any monies except those actually received by the Chargee. It is agreed that every part or lot into which the land is or may hereafter be divided does and shall stand charged with the whole money secured under the Charge and no person shall have the right to require the mortgage monies to be apportioned.

SAMPLE #5 — Continued

Obligation to Insure   **15.** The Chargor will immediately insure, unless already insured, and during the continuance of the Charge keep insured against loss or damage by fire, in such proportions upon each building as may be required by the Chargee, the buildings on the land to the amount of not less than their full insurable value in dollars of lawful money of Canada. Such insurance shall be placed with a company approved by the Chargee. Buildings shall include all buildings whether now or hereafter erected on the land, and such insurance shall include not only insurance against loss or damage by fire but also insurance against loss or damage by explosion, tempest, tornado, cyclone, lightning and all other extended perils customarily provided in insurance policies. Evidence of continuation of all such insurance having been effected shall be produced to the Chargee at least three (3) days before the expiration thereof; otherwise the Chargee may provide therefor and charge the premium paid and interest thereon at the rate provided for in the Charge to the Chargor and the same shall be payable forthwith and shall also be a charge upon the land. It is further agreed that the Chargee may at any time require any insurance of the buildings to be cancelled and new insurance effected in a company to be named by the Chargee and also of his own accord may effect or maintain any insurance herein provided for, and any amount paid by the Chargee therefor shall be payable forthwith by the Chargor with interest at the rate provided for in the Charge and shall also be a charge upon the land. Policies of insurance herein required shall provide that loss, if any, shall be payable to the Chargee as his interest may appear, subject to the standard form of mortgage clause approved by the Insurance Bureau of Canada which shall be attached to the policy of insurance.

Obligation to Repair   **16.** The Chargor will keep the land and the buildings, erections and improvements thereon, in good condition and repair according to the nature and description thereof respectively, and the Chargee may, whenever he deems necessary, by his agent enter upon and inspect the land and make such repairs as he deems necessary, and the reasonable cost of such inspection and repairs with interest at the rate provided for in the Charge shall be added to the principal amount and be payable forthwith and be a charge upon the land prior to all claims thereon subsequent to the Charge. If the Chargor shall neglect to keep the buildings, erections and improvements in good condition and repair, or commits or permits any act of waste on the land (as to which the Chargee shall be sole judge) or makes default as to any of the covenants, provisos, agreements or conditions contained in the Charge or in any charge to which this Charge is subject, all monies secured by the Charge shall, at the option of the Chargee, forthwith become due and payable, and in default of payment of same with interest as in the case of payment before maturity the powers of entering upon and leasing or selling hereby given and all other remedies herein contained may be exercised forthwith.

Extensions not to Prejudice   **17.** No extension of time given by the Chargee to the Chargor or anyone claiming under him, or any other dealing by the Chargee with the owner of the land or of any part thereof, shall in any way affect or prejudice the rights of the Chargee against the Chargor or any other person liable for the payment of the money secured by the Charge, and the Charge may be renewed by an agreement in writing at maturity for any term with or without an increased rate of interest notwithstanding that there may be subsequent encumbrances. It shall not be necessary to register any such agreement in order to retain priority for the Charge so altered over any instrument registered subsequent to the Charge. Provided that nothing contained in this paragraph shall confer any right of renewal upon the Chargor.

Non-Merger of Covenants   **18.** The taking of a judgment or judgments on any of the covenants herein shall not operate as a merger of the covenants or affect the Chargee's right to interest at the rate and times provided for in the Charge; and further that any judgment shall provide that interest thereon shall be computed at the same rate and in the same manner as provided in the Charge until the judgment shall have been fully paid and satisfied.

Change in Status   **19.** Immediately after any change or happening affecting any of the following, namely: (a) the spousal status of the Chargor, (b) the qualification of the land as a matrimonial home within the meaning of Part III of the Family Law Reform Act, and (c) the legal title or beneficial ownership of the land, the Chargor will advise the Chargee accordingly and furnish the Chargee with full particulars thereof, the intention being that the Chargee shall be kept fully informed of the names and addresses of the owner or owners for the time being of the land and of any spouse who is not an owner but who has a right of possession in the land by virtue of Section 40 of the Family Law Reform Act. In furtherance of such intention, the Chargor covenants and agrees to furnish the Chargee with such evidence in connection with any of (a), (b) and (c) above as the Chargee may from time to time request.

Date of Charge   **20.** The date of the Charge unless otherwise provided shall be the earliest date of signature by a Chargor.

Interpretation   **21.** In construing these covenants the words "Charge", "Chargee", "Chargor", "Land" and "Successor" shall have the meanings assigned to them in Section 1 of the Land Registration Reform Act, 1984 and the words "Chargor" and "Chargee" and the personal pronouns "he" and "his" relating thereto and used therewith, shall be read and construed as "Chargor" or "Chargors", "Chargee" or "Chargees", and "he", "she", "they" or "it", "his", "her", "their" or "its", respectively, as the number and gender of the parties referred to in each case require, and the number of the verb agreeing therewith shall be construed as agreeing with the said word or pronoun so substituted. And that all rights, advantages, privileges, immunities, powers and things hereby secured to the Chargor or Chargors, Chargee or Chargees, shall be equally secured to and exercisable by his, her, their or its heirs, executors, administrators and assigns, or successors and assigns, as the case may be. And that all covenants, liabilities and obligations entered into or imposed hereunder upon the Chargor or Chargors, Chargee or Chargees, shall be equally binding upon his, her, their or its heirs, executors, administrators and assigns, or successors and assigns, as the case may be, and that all such covenants and liabilities and obligations shall be joint and several. And the headings beside each paragraph herein are for reference purposes only and do not form part of the covenants herein contained.

(OVER)

SAMPLE #5 — Continued

Page 4 — SET OF STANDARD CHARGE TERMS
(Filing Date: February 22, 1985)
Filing No: 891

DYE & DURHAM CO. LIMITED
Form No. 300

ACKNOWLEDGMENT

This Set of Standard Charge Terms is included in a Charge dated the 23rd day of June 19 85 .
made by

PETER PURCHASER and PAULA PURCHASER

as Chargor(s)

To

VIOLET VENDOR

as Chargee(s)

and each Chargor hereby acknowledges receiving a copy of this Set of Standard Charge Terms before signing the Charge.

Peter Purchaser
PETER PURCHASER   Chargor

Paula Purchaser
PAULA PURCHASER

6. Privileges

As previously stated, in a mortgage situation you, the mortgagor, only have the right to redeem the property upon payment of the mortgage account and a right to possession of the property so long as the mortgage is not in default.

If you are to obtain any further rights, you will have to negotiate for them and have them set forth in the mortgage document. These are usually referred to as "privileges" and the number or strength of the privileges, of course, depends upon your bargaining position. That is, if you submit a good offer to the vendor and provide that the mortgage back to the vendor will contain various privileges, the vendor may be willing to grant these privileges in order to obtain a good price for the house.

The two most common privileges contained in residential real estate mortgages are prepayment and renewal clauses.

A mortgagee is entitled to receive income (the interest) on the principal money that is loaned over the term of the mortgage (subject to the provisions of the Mortgages Act) and thus, unless the mortgage contains a privilege of prepayment, you cannot require the mortgagee to accept more than the amount stated in the mortgage to be paid.

Unless the mortgage contains a privilege allowing you to prepay some of the principal, the mortgagee may *legally refuse* to accept an additional payment of principal. So, if you come into a small fortune, you will not be able to apply the money to the mortgage account unless either the mortgagee is willing to accept the amount or unless there is a privilege in the mortgage permitting a prepayment. An example of a prepayment privilege is contained in the mortgage reproduced as Sample #4.

The right to renewal is a common privilege. When the mortgage matures (at the end of its term), the mortgagee is entitled to demand payment of the balance due on the mortgage. Many mortgages will offer to extend the term of the mortgage, usually at a slightly higher rate of interest. However, if you are unwilling to do so, or if the mortgagee

91

is unwilling to extend the term, you will be required to pay the balance of the mortgage account in full on this date of maturity, unless the mortgage contains a privilege of renewal. An example of a renewal privilege is reproduced in the mortgage shown as Sample #4.

A third privilege, which is common in secondary financing (that is, second or third mortgages) in residential real estate is the privilege to renew or replace the first mortgage at its maturity. The following example will assist in explaining this type of privilege:

Dan and Darlene Dweller own a house with a first mortgage on it in favor of Lionel Lender which expires in 1990, at which time they will be required to pay Mr. Lender $10 000. Dan and Darlene wish to give a second mortgage to Harriet Helper in order to borrow $5 000 and this mortgage is to mature in 1992.

Now, in 1990 when the first mortgage matures, Dan and Darlene will be required to pay Lionel Lender $10 000. If, at that time, they do not have the money, they may find it necessary to arrange a further mortgage on their home. If the second mortgage given by Harriet Helper does not contain a right permitting the Dwellers to refinance their first mortgage, it will then become a first mortgage. You can see that such a provision is an important one; it is usually not difficult to obtain.

The Mortgages Act provides a right for a mortgagor to redeem the mortgage. This, in effect, is a statutory repayment privilege and a clause to this effect does not even have to be put in the mortgage.

It can be used where any principal money or interest secured by a mortgage is not, under the terms of the mortgage, payable until a time more than five years after the date of the mortgage. Any time after the expiration of five years, you may pay to the person entitled to receive the money, the amount due for principal money and interest to the time of your payment, together with *three months' further interest* in lieu of notice. No further interest is chargeable, payable or recoverable at any time thereafter on the principal money or interest due under the mortgage.

This section does not apply to any mortgage given by a joint stock company or other corporation nor to any debenture issued by any such company or corporation for the payment of which security has been given on property.

There are a few more things that you should know about what this act says. The right to redeem is a privilege of paying the *entire* mortgage account and not just part of it. The cost of exercising this right to redeem is an additional three months' interest and the section does not apply to any mortgage given by a "joint stock company or other corporation."

This last point means that the statutory right to redeem contained in the Mortgages Act is not available if you are assuming a mortgage that has been given by a corporation. This means that in most purchases of new houses, since the builder is usually a corporation, the purchaser cannot take advantage of this part of the act for purchaser "assumed" mortgages.

7. Paying off a mortgage

When you succeed in paying off a mortgage, you should make sure that all matters pertaining to the discharge of mortgage are completed. Get help from your lawyer.

Prior to making the final payment under a mortgage, you or your lawyer should write a letter to the mortgagee advising of your intentions to pay off the mortgage on a specific date and requesting a mortgage statement of the account as of that date.

In addition, you or your lawyer should request that the mortgagee prepare a discharge of the mortgage and hold it in readiness to be exchanged for the final payment. When the mortgagee has supplied the statement of account, you should compare this statement with your records in order to make sure that the final amount paid is the correct figure.

There is no obligation on a mortgagee to prepare, execute and supply such a discharge of mortgage in immediate exchange for the final payment. Most will cooperate, but some will provide the discharge only after it receives full payment, usually 30 to 45 days later.

It is in your interest to obtain and register a discharge of mortgage so that the abstract of title will reflect the removal of this encumbrance from the title. In addition, in the same manner that a mortgage is a conveyance of the legal title from the mortgagor to the mortgagee, a discharge of mortgage is a legal reconveyance of the property from the mortgagee to the mortgagor.

Since the mortgagee is not obliged to supply the discharge of mortgage, if you wish to obtain one, you will be required to pay the expenses of the mortgagee in this respect. These expenses consist of the mortgagee's legal fees (usually between $75 and $100), and your own lawyer's fees. In total, the cost for discharging a mortgage is usually between $125 and $200.

If the mortgagee refuses to execute a discharge of mortgage prior to the payment of the mortgage account in full, which the mortgagee is entitled by law to do, you are nonetheless required to continue to pay interest until the time that the mortgage account is paid in full. When this happens and the mortgagee further refuses to provide a discharge of mortgage within a reasonable time, you will have to institute an action under the Mortgages Act for an order discharging the mortgage.

This right to apply to the court for an order discharging the mortgage also exists when a mortgagee cannot be found or has died and no probate of the will has been granted or letters of administration issued, in which case you may pay the money into court as part of the proceeding. The registration of an order discharging a mortgage has the same effect as the registration of a discharge of mortgage and, thus, removes the mortgage from the title as an encumbrance and operates as a statutory reconveyance in favor of the mortgagor.

In addition to obtaining and registering a discharge of mortgage, you should also change the insurance policy. During the existence of the mortgage account, the insurance policy should contain a provision that any loss will be payable to the mortgagee, to the extent of his interest. Thus, when a mortgage is discharged, the name of the mortgagee should be deleted from the insurance policy. The insurance policy is usually amended by way of an endorsement and, in order to obtain this endorsement, a release of interest in the insurance policy should be obtained from the mortgagee at the time of discharge. This release of interest should then be forwarded to the insurance agent together with a request for the requisite endorsement.

In order to record that the mortgage has been paid off, it is desirable to register a document (i.e., a discharge of charge/mortgage) in the appropriate land registry office. In the same way as the universal form of the charge/mortgage of land document is registered regardless of whether the land is under the Land Titles Act system or the Registry Act system, a discharge of charge/mortgage is the same form that is registered in both systems to signify the release of the mortgage.

It has been common practice for the mortgagee's lawyer to prepare and produce the discharge documentation at the cost of the borrower and this continues to be the practice, notwithstanding that a recently decided case in a lower court stated that if the borrower desires, he or she may have his or her lawyer prepare the discharge documentation at the borrower's expense and the mortgagee must execute it and provide it to the borrower against payment.

8. Accounting for mortgage payments

A mortgage account will usually extend over a lengthy period of time, usually at least five years, and it is possible for a discrepancy or an error to occur at any point in time. However, if there is a dispute arising out of a discrepancy or an error, the dispute will not usually occur until the time of paying the mortgage account in full. Of course, if the mortgage term is lengthy, there is a greater possibility of an error or discrepancy occurring.

For this reason, both parties should keep an accurate list of payment dates and amounts together with a supporting record, such as the cancelled cheques, receipts and deposit slips or books. This is especially important for the mortgagor in view of the fact that if there is a problem it is his or her responsibility to establish that the mortgage has been paid in full.

To assist you in keeping track of your mortgage payments, ask your lawyer for a computerized printout showing the breakdown of each payment as between principal and interest and the balance outstanding after each payment. Some of these printouts will also show the total amount of interest paid during a particular calendar year and the daily rate of interest applicable during each month for which the schedule is obtained. This printout is most useful if you note on it the cheque number and date of each payment made under the mortgage.

Many lawyers provide this service for a minimal fee —usually $5.

9. Life insurance for your mortgage

Most real estate transactions today involve the assumption by the home owner of a substantial mortgage obligation. If you wish to make provisions to protect your family in the event of an untimely death by providing for your spouse's housing free of mortgage payments you should consider obtaining life insurance.

Since the balance of a mortgage is always reducing in amount, you should seek to obtain a policy that is also reducing in amount of coverage. This type of insurance is commonly known as "reducing term insurance," and a policy of this type will usually provide sufficient insurance coverage to retire the mortgage upon your death.

The coverage for this insurance is gradually diminished over its term. For example, a 20-year reducing term insurance policy will expire at the end of the 20-year period and, if the life insured should be living at that time, no further insurance coverage is provided. The premium for a reducing term life insurance policy is usually quite inexpensive and this type is the cheapest insurance available in the life insurance market.

If you are interested in obtaining this type of protection, you should contact your life insurance agent.

In recent years, some lending institutions have obtained a group insurance policy which insures the lives of the people who are principally responsible under a mortgage, so long as that mortgage exists, to the extent of the outstanding principal. This type of coverage obtained is relatively inexpensive and some institutions will even pay this premium instead of passing it on to the borrower. If this is of interest to you, at the time you are making the mortgage arrangements, you should ask your mortgage lending institution if it offers this insurance coverage and the cost to you of the insurance premium.

10. Government assistance

In an effort to assist the home buying public with the purchase of residential real estate, the Ontario government, through the agency of Ontario Housing Corporation, has a plan known as the H.O.M.E. Plan.

The H.O.M.E. Plan is a method of purchase of residential real estate where land and building are separated and the prospective purchaser *purchases* the building and *rents* the land from Ontario Housing Corporation for a number of years.

In addition, the purchaser will obtain an option to purchase the land from Ontario Housing Corporation upon certain terms and conditions and, therefore, has the possibility of subsequently owning the entire property. The result of the H.O.M.E. Plan is that when you initially move into your home, you do not have to pay a large down payment because you are not, at that time, buying the land from the owner. Rather, the land is owned by Ontario Housing Corporation and you merely rent the land from the corporation.

In recent years, the Ontario Housing Corporation has changed the manner in which the government assistance is provided to a prospective home owner and this is particularly relevant in the area of condominium development. Rather than instituting a H.O.M.E. Plan for a condominium development, the Ontario Housing Corporation has been willing to supply low-cost second mortgage financing for the buyers. The practical result of providing low-cost second mortgage financing is the same as the purpose of the H.O.M.E. Plan, that is, to reduce the amount of the down payment required by the purchaser, and to provide reasonable financing for the remainder of the purchase price.

The cost of this type of financing assistance varies from project to project and is usually 2% to 4% less than the conventional second mortgages available in the mortgage market. Of course, being government assistance, not everyone can obtain this type of financing. There are usually income maximums and income minimums required to permit a prospective purchaser to qualify.

These qualifications vary from project to project and are usually related to the amount of financing required. You can't apply for this type of government assistance for just any house in Ontario. It is usually supplied in groups of housing units (that is, for groups of houses, usually semi-detached, or for condominium projects) and it is provided through the builder. Thus, if you wish to get government assistance, you will have to search out the various projects for which it is available.

11. A special word about condominium financing

Obtaining a mortgage for a condominium unit has histori-cally been a more difficult task than obtaining mortgage financing for a detached or semi-detached dwelling. There are many reasons why mortgage lenders have been shy in providing funding for the condominium unit in the same way as they have been willing to provide mortgage funding for other types of housing; however, there is one area of concern about condominium units to mortgage lenders that is not widely known to condominium owners or con-dominium purchasers. This concern is about litigation or potential litigation between the condominium corporation and the condominium developer. Over the past several years, there have been many such lawsuits involving many millions of dollars and mortgage lenders have shown extreme reluctance to become financially involved in a project that is burdened with this type of situation. It is for this reason that mortgage lenders do (and potential purchasers should) insist upon reviewing the condominium corporation's financial statements before making a commitment — the financial statements of the condominium corporation usually prove to be a good indicator of the existence, nature and severity of any problem involving this type of litigation.

7

SELLING YOUR HOME

a. INTRODUCTION

As a home owner, you know what it cost you to buy your home and you know what you have had to pay for maintenance. However, there are factors relating to the marketing of a home that you may not be aware of.

Generally speaking, the residential real estate market in Ontario over the past several years has been extremely active and many homes have greatly increased in value over a short period of time.

After you have decided to sell your home, three other matters must then be decided before the house is put on the market.

An asking price must be determined. Of course, every vendor wishes to obtain the best possible price for his or her home but, on the other hand, you will not wish to put such a high price on the house that prospective purchasers are discouraged from inspecting the property. Price levels are most easily determined by finding out what other similar houses in the area have sold for. Over a period of years most home owners acquire fairly accurate knowledge regarding the selling price of homes in their area. Short of this, you can find many people who are knowledgeable in real estate to suggest a market price. If you use an agent, he or she will, of course, be of assistance here.

You must decide how you are going to be paid. Most houses are owned subject to at least one mortgage and you will have to consider the following alternatives:

(a) You can ask for cash for your equity and allow the purchaser to take over the first mortgage (commonly called a "cash to mortgage" sale); in this case the purchaser will assume the first mortgage.

(b) You can pay off the first mortgage and then take back a first mortgage yourself from the purchaser.

(c) You can have the purchaser assume the first mortgage and take back a second mortgage for a portion of the remainder of the purchase price.

This matter is not always determined solely by the vendor's desires. In many cases, the decision is made based upon your requirements for your new housing situation. For example, if you require a great deal of cash in order to buy a new home, you will probably wish to sell the home for cash to the mortgage. On the other hand, if you are moving into an apartment, you may wish to retain an investment in the home being sold in order to earn an attractive amount of interest and, in this situation, will be in a position to consider the other alternatives.

Last, but certainly not least, you must find the right buyer for your home. In other words, you must consider how best to approach the real estate market.

Today, the majority of residential real estate transactions occur through the use of a real estate agent. The real estate agent performs two services for the vendor. First, because the agent is in constant contact with the real estate market, he or she can advise you on pricing the property. Second, the real estate agent has ready access to prospective customers. Thus, if you wish to obtain a quick sale of your home, it is probably advisable to employ the services of an agent.

The major disadvantage to the use of a real estate agent is the fact that the commission charged may represent a large amount of the money. An agent usually charges a commission of 3% to 10% depending on the area and the type of service offered. You are liable to pay this immediately upon completion of the sale. Thus, if the amount of money received from the sale of the home is an important factor to you, you may wish to attempt to sell your home without employing a real estate agent.

There are alternatives to employing a real estate agent and in today's active market many home owners are finding that the agent is not needed to find a purchaser. The common alternatives to using an agent are as follows:

(a) Put a sign on your front lawn. The only cost will be the price of the sign.

(b) Place an advertisement in the local newspaper. You will have to pay the cost of the advertisement, but this gives you wider coverage.

(c) In recent years, several types of services to introduce prospective purchasers to prospective vendors have been established and you can seek to sell your home through one of these services. A fee is charged for this service; however, the fee is usually substantially less than the commission that would be payable to a real estate agent.

b. WHAT DOES A REAL ESTATE AGENT DO?

Because land is a commodity bought and sold and because expertise is often required to find a buyer, there are specialists whose function it is to seek purchasers for real estate on the market.

These specialists can help establish the value of your property because they know how much similar property sold for in similar circumstances.

Also, they advertise the property for you to help you find a buyer. The main function, then, of the agent is to bring together buyers and sellers of real estate.

Because an agent earns money on the basis of a commission for helping to sell your property, he or she will not act for you unless you enter into a binding agreement. This is called the "listing agreement" and is discussed in the next section.

The real estate agent is usually paid by the vendor of the home on the basis of a percentage of the sale price. For this reason, it is in the mutual interest of both you and the agent to obtain the highest possible price for your home. However, since the agent does not earn any income until a sale is transacted, he or she may encourage you to accept a lower price for your home in order to sell it.

In many situations, two real estate agents will both work on the same transaction. This will usually occur when one of the agents has your listing agreement and the second agent has contact with a prospective purchaser. It is a common fallacy that the real estate agent who has the contact with the purchaser is the agent of the purchaser. In fact, this is not true since it is the vendor who pays both agents.

It must be remembered that a real estate agent depends upon the sale of property for his or her livelihood and, accordingly, will be pushing hard to sell your house. This is a valuable service in a buyer's market. However, if it is a seller's market, an agent may be somewhat superfluous.

c. WHAT YOU SHOULD KNOW ABOUT THE LISTING AGREEMENT

The real estate agent will usually require you to sign a contract which entitles the agent to a commission. This agreement is insisted upon because the Real Estate and Business Brokers Act provides that no action may be brought for the payment of a commission for the sale of real estate unless the agreement is in writing and signed by the person who is responsible for paying the commission.

This does not mean the real estate agent does not become entitled to the commission if the agreement pertaining to the commission is not in writing; however, if the agreement is not in writing, the real estate agent, in case of non-payment, is prohibited from bringing an action. The practical difference here is that if a commission is paid following an oral agreement, the agent will be entitled to keep it.

There are three types of listing agreements available in the modern real estate market. These are the open listing, the exclusive listing and the multiple listing.

Under an open listing you, the vendor, agree to pay the real estate agent a specified rate of commission, usually the lowest rate of commission charged in the real estate market, upon the real estate agent obtaining a purchaser for the property. The real estate agent in an open listing does not have exclusive authority over the property, and you may enter into several open listing agreements with other agents.

An exclusive listing is similar in form to the open listing as far as describing the property concerned; however, the rate of commission under an exclusive listing is usually slightly higher than the rate under an open listing.

Under an exclusive listing, you would give the real estate agent the exclusive right to sell your property for a specified period of time and, if the property is sold by anyone else during this period of time or if the property is sold to someone who is introduced by the real estate agent within a period of time after the expiry of the listing agreement, the real estate agent is entitled to the commission. A real estate agent will usually work harder on an exclusive listing because he or she stands a better chance of earning a commission.

The third type of listing agreement is the multiple listing, where several of the real estate agents in a specific area agree to pool their resources by forming an association and, by so doing, have a larger supply of homes to show prospective purchasers and have a larger supply of prospective purchasers to introduce to willing vendors.

The multiple listing usually contains the same factual information as provided under an open or an exclusive listing but, in addition, it may contain a photograph of the property.

The rate of real estate commission under a multiple listing is usually higher than the rate included in the exclusive listing, the reason being that most sales under a multiple listing involve collaboration between more than one real estate agent and, thus, the sharing of the real estate commission. In addition, the expenses involved with a multiple listing are usually higher than the expenses incurred in the other types of listing.

This type of listing, because of its exposure to all other real estate agents in the association, provides the greatest amount of exposure to the purchasing public and is the most useful way of selling a home if you are in a hurry.

A word of caution — many listing agreements and forms of offer to purchase state that a commission is payable for arranging a contract (that is, even if the sale does not go through). A prudent vendor, when signing such a listing agreement or offer to purchase should add a sentence such as "Commission payable only if and when the transaction is completed" in order to protect against this potential liability.

d. DISCLOSURE BY THE VENDOR TO THE PURCHASER

If there is a default on the part of the purchaser, the vendor will retain all of his or her rights under the agreement. These rights consist of one of the following remedies:

(a) Forfeiture of the deposit of the purchaser

(b) The right to sue the purchaser for specific performance to complete the transaction which means the purchaser will be required to complete the transaction

(c) The right to sue the purchaser for damages suffered by the vendor as a result of the failure of the purchaser to complete the transaction

On the other hand, if the transaction is not completed due to the default of the vendor, he or she may be required to return the deposit or may be liable to an action by the purchaser to complete the transaction (specific performance) with an abatement of the purchase price and/or damages.

In order to be protected, it is necessary for the vendor to disclose all the relevant information with regard to the title to the property. For example, if the property is subject to an easement, a right of way or other restriction on the title or an encroachment by neighboring property, it should be disclosed in the agreement.

This disclosure of imperfections in the title to the real estate does not include problems relating to the actual house. For example, while a survey defect should be disclosed in the agreement, a broken window need not be mentioned. The reason for this is that the doctrine of "caveat emptor" (buyer beware) applies to the sale of older homes.

e. WHAT ABOUT THE DEPOSIT?

There is no legal requirement for a purchaser to provide a large or substantial deposit or even any deposit at all. Over a period of years this practice has arisen as a means of indicating the purchaser's good faith.

The size of the deposit can be flexible. As a matter of practice a figure in the amount of around 6% of the total price is considered standard. You, the vendor will want as large a deposit as possible because, as previously stated, a purchaser who fails to complete may forfeit the deposit made and, accordingly, the larger the amount of deposit, the greater the incentive for the purchaser to complete.

A further reason for the requirement of a substantial deposit relates to the fact that, if an agent is involved, he or she will receive the deposit on your behalf and retain it in a trust account until the transaction is completed. After completion, the real estate agent applies the deposit toward the commission payable. Thus, it is not uncommon for an agent to attempt to obtain a deposit approximately the amount of the real estate commission.

The trust account of a real estate agent is governed by the provisions of the Real Estate and Business Brokers Act and the real estate agent cannot disburse these trust funds until one of the following events occurs:

(a) The transaction is completed.

(b) Both the vendor and the purchaser provide the real estate agent with the same direction as to the disbursement of the funds.

(c) A court order is obtained directing the real estate agent to disburse the funds in a certain manner.

If the deposit is paid directly to the vendor, there is no requirement upon the vendor to hold these monies in trust but, rather, the vendor is free to use the money as he or she pleases, unless the agreement of purchase and sale provides otherwise.

In recent years, deposits and interest rates have been substantial. Accordingly, it is not uncommon to place a clause in the agreement of purchase and sale to the effect that the agent will invest the deposit in a term deposit certificate until the date of closing and, on closing, the interest earned on the deposit is to be paid to either party. Unless a direction to this effect is given to the real estate agent, the agent is not entitled to earn interest on the deposit for anyone, including the agent.

f. THE DOWN PAYMENT

The down payment refers to the amount of the deposit plus the additional amount to be paid in cash by the purchaser on closing. In other words, the down payment is the amount of the sale price, less the amount of mortgage financing.

The amount of the down payment will not be relevant if you are selling your home on a cash to mortgage basis. On the other hand, if you are taking back a mortgage, the amount of the down payment will be of some concern. In this situation, you will wish to make sure that the purchaser has a sufficient interest in the property to induce the purchaser to meet the mortgage obligations.

It is a common rule of thumb for secondary financing (which refers to financing subsequent to a first mortgage), that the owner of the property should have an interest in the property at least equal to the amount of the secondary financing. For example, if a property is being sold for $40 000, of which $30 000 is outstanding on a first mortgage, the secondary financing, (perhaps the second mortgage taken back by the vendor) should not be greater than $5 000.

Of course, if you are taking back a first mortgage on the property, this does not apply. Instead you must consider the amount of money being invested in the property by the new purchaser compared to the amount of the total purchase price.

In all situations where you are considering a mortgage back, you should collect in cash (by way of down payment) an amount at least equal to the amount you would have to expend in claiming the repossession and reselling in the event of default by the purchaser.

This margin should be sufficient to cover interest for six months to one year plus the cost of having to re-sell the property. For example, if you sell your home for $40 000 on which there is a $30 000 first mortgage, and take back a second mortgage of $6 000, the margin will be $4 000. This must be sufficient to cover all of the costs of a subsequent sale of the property, such as real estate commission, insurance, realty taxes, legal fees and disbursements and interest on the first and second mortgages.

g. PAYING OFF A PRE-EXISTING MORTGAGE

We have already discussed the problem where a vendor is required to pay off a pre-existing mortgage prior to or at the time of closing of the transaction. Technically you, the vendor in this situation, are required to discharge the mortgage out of your own funds and obtain and register a discharge of the mortgage on or before closing. However, it is a common conveyancing practice for the vendor and purchaser to agree that the money to be used for paying off the pre-existing mortgage will be paid out of the funds paid by the purchaser on the closing.

This arrangement is usually made through the parties' lawyers in such a way that one of the lawyers will be responsible for paying this money to the mortgagee (lender) and obtaining and registering the discharge of mortgage following the closing of the transaction.

If you must pay off a pre-existing mortgage, you or your lawyer must first obtain a mortgage statement from the mortgagee in order to ascertain the amount required to be paid. This amount should be checked against your own records and any discrepancy cleared up prior to closing date.

h. ARE YOU TAKING BACK A MORTGAGE?

The factors to be considered by the vendor in taking back a mortgage have been discussed in section f.

The important thing to remember is that if you are taking back a mortgage, the terms of this mortgage must be described in complete detail in the agreement of purchase and sale. This includes the amount of the mortgage, the interest rate, the term, the period during which the interest is compounded, the instalment periods, the instalment dates and any privileges to be included in the mortgage. You will note that the agreement of purchase and sale reproduced as Sample #2 discusses the terms of the mortgage back in a brief but concise manner.

i. TRANSFER OF POSSESSION

Unless a provision to the contrary is contained in the agreement of purchase and sale, the vendor of a property will be required to transfer possession of the home on the date of closing. This, of course, is subject to any tenancies of the property which you and the purchaser have agreed will be assumed by the purchaser.

You will have to make sure that you will be in a position to give up possession on the date of closing. If you are using the money from the sale of the old property in order to complete the purchase of new property, you must obtain the same date of closing for both transactions and be prepared to move from the old house to the new house on the date of closing.

The physical transfer of possession is usually accomplished by the vendor, or his or her lawyer, giving a key to the purchaser or his or her lawyer. Most lawyers will require that you give a key to the lawyer so that it may be delivered on the closing, at the same time as the transfer of funds from the purchaser's lawyer.

Many vendors will be willing to give a prospective purchaser a key prior to the date of closing in order to permit him or her to move some belongings into the premises. There are dangers here, however, and it is recommended that this not be done without a prior discussion with your lawyer.

j. INSURANCE

Fire insurance policies apply to individual homes. For this reason, one does not usually have a policy transferred to a new home. To take care of this, the standard form purchase offer provides that the insurance policy will be transferred from the vendor to the purchaser on the closing of the transaction and that the premium will be adjusted. Fire insurance is considered by many lawyers to be an item of very high priority in a real estate transaction and, of course, it is a matter of great importance to all parties concerned.

Fire insurance should be in an amount sufficient to replace the dwelling if it is totally destroyed. In determining your fire insurance requirements, keep in mind that land cannot, of course, be destroyed by fire and the amount of the insurance coverage should usually be the replacement value of the property, less the value of the land.

There are several types of fire insurance policies available in today's insurance market and you should discuss your individual requirements with your insurance agent. A common provision in fire insurance policies requires that the owner of the property must advise the insurance company if the property is to be vacant for a period longer than 10 to 15 days. Thus, if you are selling your property and moving out 10 or 15 days before the closing date, a letter should be written to the insurance agent or company advising them that the property will be vacant for a specified period of time and an endorsement to the insurance policy, commonly called a vacancy permit, should be obtained. There is usually no charge by the insurance company for issuing a vacancy permit.

Insurance covering the risk of personal liability or damage to the contents of the home may be transferred from one dwelling to another dwelling and it is not common for a vendor to transfer this type of insurance coverage to the purchaser.

However, in many insurance policies in common use today, especially the types of policies that are designated as home owner's policies, the three types of coverage (fire, personal liability, and contents coverage) are covered under one policy.

Since the liability and contents portion of this type of policy cannot be assigned to a purchaser and since many insurance companies will not agree to divide the coverage between the fire portion, on the one hand, and the contents and liability portion, on the other hand, the parties in real estate transactions usually make their own individual arrangements for insurance.

k. TENANCIES

In many real estate transactions, the parties agree that the conveyance will be subject to the tenancy of one or more tenants involving all or part of the dwelling. As previously mentioned, a purchaser in this situation will attempt to obtain acknowledgements from the various tenants by having the vendor agree to obtain these acknowledgements prior to closing.

If there is any doubt as to the tenants' willingness to sign an acknowledgement, the vendor should be protected in the offer by agreeing to *attempt to obtain* an acknowledgement rather than agreeing to *actually obtain* the acknowledgement.

If this presents a problem to the purchaser, the vendor may attempt to obtain the acknowledgements personally and, if unable to produce acknowledgements from all of the tenants, he or she will provide a statutory declaration with respect to the terms of the tenancies of the various tenants who have not supplied acknowledgements.

In addition to the tenants' acknowledgements, the purchaser will require a notice from the vendor to the tenant or tenants advising that the property has been sold and that all future payments of rent should be made payable to the new purchaser. This "direction" is usually produced on the closing of the transaction.

The right to receive rent is determined as of the date of closing and, of course, the vendor is entitled to rent only up until that date and the purchaser is entitled to rent thereafter.

111

l. PLANNING ACT

If the vendor is selling the whole of a lot on a registered plan of subdivision, it is unlikely that any problems will be encountered with regard to the Planning Act. However, if the vendor's property consists of part of a lot on a registered subdivision and if the vendor retains an ownership interest in property abutting the land being sold, the vendor must obtain the consent of the local Land Division Committee or Committee of Adjustment or, if there is none, the Minister of Municipal Affairs. There are two factors concerning this consent that should be noted by the vendor.

(a) An application for consent under Section 49 of the Planning Act (commonly called an application for a severance) involves some expense, including the cost of obtaining a survey, submitting the application, and obtaining legal assistance at the hearing of the application.

(b) The application for consent may be refused. To be protected, a vendor should include in the agreement of purchase and sale that the vendor will apply for the necessary consent to severance and, if the application is refused, the vendor will then have no liability to the purchaser.

If an application for a consent to severance is required, it must be remembered that this application will take at least six or eight weeks until a decision is made and until the appeal period has passed. Thus, the date of the closing of the transaction should be established accordingly.

Finally, regarding the cost of the application for consent to severance, you should consult a lawyer before signing the offer in order to obtain some indication of what this cost will be.

m. HOW TO ACCEPT AN OFFER TO PURCHASE

Most standard forms of offers to purchase contain a clause at the bottom for signature by the vendor. This clause has two effects:

(a) The vendor accepts the offer of the purchaser and, by so doing, becomes bound by the terms of the offer.

(b) There is an agreement between the vendor and the real estate agent for the payment of the real estate commission and an outline of the mechanics of this payment.

Regarding the commission, you should add a provision that the commission will be payable if, and only if, the transaction is completed. If no real estate agent is involved in the transaction, this should be deleted from the offer and initialled by the parties.

In considering an offer to purchase, you should make sure that the offer is in strict accordance with the facts relating to the dwelling. In addition, if the offer imposes various obligations on you, you should be certain that you will be able to comply with these obligations within the required time.

If there are matters contained that are warranties, representations, covenants or provisions that must be dealt with after the time of closing, you should ensure that these items are changed so that they are concluded before closing and are actually a condition of the closing. In this way you will not find yourself on the end of a lawsuit for damages after you thought the transaction was completed.

As mentioned before, if you wish to change any clause in the offer, you may do so by making the necessary change, initialling the change, and, of course, signing the offer to purchase.

In addition to making the change, you will also have to review and, perhaps, make a change to the clause (usually in the standard form) that states how long the offer is available for acceptance and by whom acceptance is to be made. These changes will constitute a counter-offer, which the purchaser may accept. When the vendor makes a change in an offer to purchase, this counter-offer is commonly called a mark-back or sign-back.

n. ARE YOU SELLING UNDER AN AGREEMENT FOR SALE?

An agreement for sale is a different method of selling from the normal method of conveying title on the closing date. In an agreement for sale, the purchaser obtains possession of the property on closing date but does not receive *title* to the property until all money owing to the vendor has been paid. When the vendor has received *all* of the money owing to him or her, the vendor will convey title to the property to the purchaser and the purchaser will then become the owner of the property subject to the pre-existing mortgages that have been placed by the vendor.

The basic difference between an agreement for sale and the normal transfer is the time at which the title passes from the vendor to the purchaser. In both situations, the purchaser obtains possession of the dwelling at the date that is agreed upon. In addition, in both situations, the purchaser can arrange subsequent financing on the security of the real property.

However, there is a difference in the type of financing. If there is an offer or agreement of purchase and sale, the subsequent financing will be arranged by way of a mortgage. If there is an agreement for sale, the financing will be arranged by way of an "assignment of the agreement for sale" containing a provision for the re-assignment back to the purchaser following repayment of the financing.

It is of great potential benefit to you to convey title by this method because, if there are foreclosure proceedings, you already have title and merely need an order for possession. The whole procedure is made easier and simpler. However, while commonly in use in other provinces, it is not used frequently in Ontario.

o. SELLING A CONDOMINIUM UNIT

Condominium units, as well as co-operative units, are relatively recent developments in the real estate market and, at the present time, it is difficult to know whether this type of housing is more or less easily sold than traditional housing.

The sale of a condominium unit involves all of the matters previously mentioned with regard to the sale of a house plus additional matters.

The safe rule of thumb here is that you should make available to the purchaser *all* information relating to the condominium including copies of the declaration, by-laws, management agreement, insurance trust agreement and any other notices received from the condominium corporation.

By so doing, the prospective purchaser can make himself or herself aware of all of the requirements contained in this documentation prior to submitting an offer to purchase. To further protect yourself, you should insert a clause into the offer to the effect that the purchaser has read and understands the condominium documentation and agrees to comply with their provisions.

You also should advise the purchaser of all financial obligations arising out of ownership of a unit, such as contributions for common expenses, contingency funds and reserve funds. Full disclosure here is especially important when you are taking a mortgage back because only in this way can you ensure that the purchaser will make an informed decision regarding his or her ability to handle the monthly payments.

8

GETTING A LAWYER

a. INTRODUCTION

In many real estate transactions, either or both of the parties do not obtain legal advice until after the agreement of purchase and sale has been signed.

The agreement of purchase and sale is probably the most important legal document in a real estate transaction. And since the purchase of a house is probably the largest investment of your life, this agreement may well be the most important document you will ever sign.

If there is a single lesson to be learned from this book, it is the importance of retaining competent legal advice before signing anything. The best way to find a competent lawyer is to consult friends and acquaintances. If you can find no leads there, you may consult the yellow pages.

A lawyer may be recommended to you by a real estate agent. We do not recommend this practice and suggest you will be better served through independent advice.

Before retaining a lawyer you should first determine that he or she does real estate work and secondly, what the price range will be. You may not be able to get an exact figure, but depending on the price range of the house, you should get a ball park figure. Normal charges for a house transfer are discussed below. If you do not feel satisfied with a particular lawyer, simply say you would like to think it over and excuse yourself and, then, try another.

It is suggested that a prudent practice in purchasing real estate is to have the real estate agent discuss the property and the terms of the contract with the prospective purchaser's legal advisor *prior* to preparation of the offer and, subsequently, to have the document reviewed by the lawyer prior to signing it.

It must be remembered that your legal adviser is merely that — a legal adviser. Thus, you cannot expect a lawyer to provide advice regarding the business aspects of a transaction. A lawyer will normally assist you by providing protection for your rights but will not provide assistance in furthering your business interests in the transaction. It is for this reason that the answer to some of your questions may be, "That is a question you will have to answer yourself."

b. A LAWYER OR A NOTARY PUBLIC?

Many people do not realize that there is a difference between a lawyer and a notary public. A lawyer in Ontario may become a notary public merely by applying to be a notary public; however, a notary public is not necessarily a lawyer.

A notary is able to transfer title by preparing the required documentation in a real estate transaction and swearing the necessary affidavits required in the transaction. However, a notary public is not formally qualified to provide a legal opinion.

A person who retains a lawyer will usually pay extra for competent legal advice. Specifically, a lawyer makes various searches and, on the basis of these searches, is able to provide an opinion on the quality of the title. In view of the fact that the transaction represents a major undertaking for the purchaser, it is usually worth the extra fee to use a lawyer as long as the job is done. In a sale transaction, the services of a lawyer are required in two instances.

(a) When the purchaser or lawyer encounters a problem (called a "requisition"). In this instance, a knowledge of the law is usually required.

(b) When there are encumbrances such as a mortgage on the title to the property that must be removed at the time of closing. For example, if the vendor has a mortgage on the property of $10 000 and has agreed to sell the house to the purchaser for $25 000 entirely in cash, the vendor is responsible for obtaining and registering a discharge of the $10 000 mortgage. A purchaser is not required to accept title with this encumbrance, even if the vendor promises to pay the $10 000 out of the balance due on closing. Thus, if part of the sale price is required to be used to discharge an encumbrance such as this at or following closing, the assistance of a lawyer will probably be required.

c. WHAT WILL A LAWYER CHARGE?

The lawyer's bill is comprised of two items: the lawyer's fees for services and the disbursements.

The disbursements charged by a lawyer are those expenditures that the lawyer has made on your behalf such as expenses incurred for various searches and registrations required to complete the transaction. These disbursements must actually be spent by the lawyer.

A lawyer's fee is based on a number of matters, including the purchase price of the property, the amount of time spent on the transaction, the difficulty of the particular real estate transaction and other factors.

One of these other factors is the tariff established by the local law association of the district or county in which the lawyer practises. Tariffs are referred to as guidelines by some people and price fixing schedules by others.

Whichever it is called, the tariff is a guideline provided to the members of the law association to indicate "proper" charges for the average transaction.

The tariff is not binding and you will often find lawyers who charge less than the tariff. Many will follow it, however. To give you an idea of the fees outlined in a tariff, the County of York Law Association tariff of suggested fees for either a purchase or sale of other than commercial properties is as follows:

> (a) Purchase of Residential Properties (including recreational property for personal use.) Purchaser's solicitor for reviewing executed agreement of purchase and sale (but not including negotiating or drawing agreement) and advising in connection therewith, investigating title, making requisitions on title, searching for arrears of realty and all other

taxes and rates constituting statutory liens, searching for executions, reviewing transfer, preparation of one charge given back, reviewing statement of adjustments and examining survey (if available) or otherwise advising the client with respect to the significance thereof, making zoning and building by-law inquiries, and searching for work orders, discussing with the purchaser all matters relating to title, zoning and statement of adjustments, attending on execution of documents, attending the closing, giving opinion on title, reporting and all other services necessarily incidental thereto;

On sale price of the property (inclusive of encumbrances to be assumed)

$60 000 or less .... $ 600

On the excess over $60 000, up to a total sale price of $250 000 between 1/4 and 1/2 of 1 per cent of the said excess, to be determined by the time spent, the complexity of the transaction and the amount involved:

The total not ordinarily to exceed $1 200

On the excess over $250 000 additional fees may be charged, the amount thereof to be determined by the time spent, the complexity of the transaction and the amount involved.

(b) Purchaser of Residential Condominium Units. Purchaser's Solicitor for reviewing agreement of purchase and sale (but not including negotiating or drawing agreement) and accompanying documents, including reviewing declaration, by-laws, management contract, insurance trust agreement and all other condominium documentation, advising in connection therewith, investigating title and checking the description, searching for arrears of realty and other taxes and rates constituting statutory liens, making zoning and building by-law inquiries, searching for work orders, examining condominium unit plan, making requisitions on title and concerning the contract, reviewing transfer, obtaining and reviewing statement from condominium corporations as to financial condition, reviewing statement of adjustments, preparing charge given back (if any), considering and advising about occupancy agreement and discussing with the purchaser all matters relating to title, zoning, condominium registration and adjustments, and attending on closing, attending on execution of documents, advising about common expenses, insurance coverage, boundary limits of condominium unit and responsibility and participation in condominium corporation, giving opinion on title, reporting, and all other services necessarily incidental thereto: on the sale price of the unit (inclusive of encumbrances to be assumed) .... same fees as in (a).

(c) Sale of Residential Properties (including sale of recreational property for personal use). Vendor's solicitor for reviewing executed agreement of purchase and sale (but not including negotiating or drawing agreement) and advising in connection therewith, preparing transfer, answering requisitions on title, preparing statement of adjustments and advising in connection therewith, reviewing charge taken back (if any), attending on execution of documentation, attending the closing and completing the sale, reporting to client and all other services necessarily incidental thereto:

On the sale price of the property (inclusive of encumbrances to be assumed) .... 3/4 of the fees as in item (a).

(d) Sale of Residential Condominium Unit. Vendor's solicitor for reviewing executed agreement of purchase and sale (but not including negotiating or drawing agreement) and advising in connection therewith, supplying copies of declaration, by-laws, management contract, insurance trust agreement, up-to-date insurance certificate, preparing transfer of title, answering requisitions, preparing statement of adjustments and advising in connection therewith, reviewing charge taken back (if any), attending on execution of documentation, attending and closing and completing the sale, reporting to client and all other services necessarily incidental thereto:

On the sale price of the property (inclusive of encumbrances to be assumed) .... 3/4 of the fees as in item (a).

Thus, on a real estate transaction where the purchase price is $100 000, the County of York Law Association tariff is between $700 and $800, plus disbursements. For a $150 000 home, the suggested fee is between $825 and $1 050, plus disbursements. The same tariff applies to both the vendor and the purchaser and if the property is a condominium unit, the fees are three-quarters of these amounts.

Each of the lawyers in the transaction (i.e., the lawyer for the purchaser and the lawyer for the vendor) will charge legal fees to their respective clients and these legal fees do not include the disbursements, which will be an additional charge to the vendor and to the purchaser. Sample #6 shows a statement of account (bill) for a purchaser and Sample #7 shows a statement of account for a vendor. They usually have different lawyers representing each of them. In rare circumstances, the same lawyer may represent both of them but, in these cases, it is difficult for a lawyer to represent both clients without having a conflict of interest.

If you are unhappy about your bill and if the fee was not a fee that was agreed upon in advance, you can have your bill "assessed." This procedure used to be called "taxation." This procedure is conducted before an official of the Supreme Court of Ontario, called an Assessment Officer, who will hear all the matters involved in the solicitor's bill and the problems therewith felt by the client, after which the Assessment Officer will determine if a fair amount has been charged by the solicitor and, if not, will decide what amount is a fair amount to be paid in all of the circumstances of the transaction. It is important to note that you must file all of the initial paperwork with the office of the Assessment Officer within 30 days after presentation of the lawyer's bill, otherwise you may be refused the opportunity of having the bill assessed.

You may negotiate the fee in advance, although it is difficult to determine the exact fee at the start of the transaction, because the lawyer is not aware of all of the difficulties that may be encountered during the transaction. However, you should get an estimate or ball park figure depending upon the complexity of the matter.

Many people feel embarrassed to ask for a quote from a lawyer. There is no reason for reluctance on your part to ask for a quote. After all, you will need to properly organize your financial affairs so that the transaction will be closed as smoothly as possible.

d. SERVICES PROVIDED BY THE PURCHASER'S LAWYER

1. How is title to be registered?

One of the first matters to be discussed with your lawyer is how the title is to be registered. In residential real estate

SAMPLE #6
STATEMENT OF ACCOUNT TO PURCHASER

Mr. and Mrs. P. Purchaser
1234 Any Street
Toronto, Ontario
M0M 0M0   July 7th, 198-

In Account With

BARRISTER AND SOLICITOR
Barristers and Solicitors
100 Legal Lane
Toronto, Ontario
M0M 0M1

TO OUR FEES HEREIN		$535.00
DISBURSEMENTS		
Paid for tax certificate	$ 5.00	
Paid for search of title	11.50	
Paid for photocopies	12.00	
Paid for mortgage schedule	3.00	
Paid for subsearch of title	1.00	
Paid to register Deed	10.00	
Paid as Land Transfer Tax	235.20	
Paid as Retail Sales Tax on your purchase of chattels	70.00	
Total Disbursements	$347.70	$347.70
TOTAL FEES AND DISBURSEMENTS		$882.70

THIS IS OUR ACCOUNT

BARRISTER AND SOLICITOR

PER: <u>(signed) *J. a. Barrister*</u>

E. & O. E.

SAMPLE #7
STATEMENT OF ACCOUNT TO VENDOR

Mr. V. Vendor
629571 Some Street   July 7th, 198-
Scarborough, Ontario

In Account With
ME AND YOU
Barristers and Solicitors
5678 Our Street
Toronto, Ontario

RE: VENDOR SALE TO PURCHASER,
1234 ANY STREET, TORONTO

TO OUR FEES HEREIN		$425.00
DISBURSEMENTS		
Paid for subsearch of title	$ .75	
Paid for photocopies	2.50	
Paid to register		
second Mortgage	10.00	
Paid for loan schedule	1.00	
Total Disbursements	$14.25	14.25
TOTAL FEES AND DISBURSEMENTS		$439.25

STATEMENT OF TRUST ACCOUNT
Received as proceeds of sale
of second Mortgage $6 200.00

Applied toward account of
Vendor purchase from New
Builders Limited,
629571 Some Street,
Scarborough,   Ontario   5 760.75

Amount on Hand $439.25

Less our Total Fees
and Disbrusements $439.25

BALANCE DUE AND
OWING TO US   NIL

THIS IS OUR ACCOUNT,

ME AND YOU

PER: (signed) *I. C. You .*

E. & O. E.

transactions, except when the property is owned by a builder or developer, it is rare to find the title registered in any name other than that of the husband or wife or both of them together.

If you are married, the first decision to be made is whether the property will be owned by one of you or both of you. Some of the factors to consider in this decision are:

(a) Who is supplying the money for the down payment?
(b) Who will be primarily responsible for the payment of the mortgage instalment?
(c) What is the likelihood of success of the marriage?
(d) The exposure of liability of each of the individuals
(e) The income tax bracket of the individuals

In any given situation (for example, when one of the spouses is in business), one of these factors may be paramount and overriding to such an extent that it determines the manner in which title is to be registered.

For example, if a couple has a successful marriage and each has contributed an equal amount of money to the purchase, but the husband is in a very risky business, the last factor dictates that the property should be registered in the wife's name alone and that any payments toward the home that are made by the husband will be by way of a gift to the wife. In this manner, the home will be protected from attack by the business creditors of the husband.

The likelihood of the marriage being successful is another factor to be given serious consideration. If there is any doubt as to its success, it would be foolish for the contributing partner to either become excluded from or give up part of the ownership; once it is gone it could be very difficult, if at all possible, to retrieve.

Even if, for example, the home is registered in the name of one of the spouses, the other spouse has rights under the Family Law Act of Ontario that would prevent the spouse that is holding title to sell or mortgage the property without the consent of the non-titled spouse.

The Family Law Act deals with many aspects of the spousal relationship, including the ownership and right to possession of the matrimonial home and other family assets. A lengthy discussion of this act is beyond the scope of this book and any problems or questions in this area of the law should be referred to a lawyer practising in that field. However, the theory of this act is that, except where there is an agreement between the spouses to the contrary and except in the most rare circumstances, spouses should share equally any property or other benefits that they gain during the time of the spousal relationship.

The decision as to the manner in which the title is to be registered does not necessarily have to be made prior to the signing of the agreement of purchase and sale. This can, in most instances, be changed prior to the completion of the transaction.

In my experience, most married couples want the title registered in the names of both of the spouses, on the theory that the property of each is the property of the other and that the marriage is a stable one.

The two most common methods of multiple ownership are *tenancy in common* and *joint tenancy*. In each of these types of ownership, each spouse is the sole owner of an *undivided one-half interest* in the whole of the property. Thus, the two spouses comprise the whole of the ownership of the property but neither spouse can say "This is my half and that is your half."

The difference between joint tenancy and tenancy in common is that a joint tenancy has the *right of survivorship* associated with it. This means that if one spouse dies the other automatically becomes entitled to the whole of the property.

Contrast this with a tenancy in common where, upon the death of the first spouse, the undivided one-half interest of that spouse passes to that spouse's heirs in accordance with the will of the spouse, which may or may not include the other spouse. If the spouse does not leave a will, the family home may or may not pass to the other spouse, and it may have to go through the courts.

2. The survey

Your lawyer should request a copy of the survey from the vendor, who is obligated to provide it if there is one. Upon receiving the survey, your lawyer will examine the information shown and determine whether there are any problems. Your lawyer will discuss these with you in order to decide on the proper course of action.

Many municipalities offer a service for a fee where they will examine a copy of the sketch of survey and advise whether the information shown complies with the relevant by-laws of the municipality.

In a condominium project, a survey of the entire condominium project will be filed in the appropriate Land Registry Office.

3. Searching the title

Your lawyer should make a search of the title being claimed by the vendor. Under the standard offer or agreement of purchase and sale, the vendor is responsible for conveying a good and marketable (clear) title unless the contrary is stated.

In Ontario there are two systems of registration of titles to land: the Registry Act system and the Land Titles Act system (see Sample #8). Land is registered only under one of these systems. Each system is governed by an act and both of these acts require that dealings with the land be registered in order to provide notice to the general public.

By providing a central location for the registration of interests in land, and by requiring that interests in land, in order to be effective, must be registered, the law has reduced the possibility of fraud or misrepresentation. Both of these acts provide that a document that is not registered has no effect against people whose documents are registered.

It is vital to the protection of your property interest that the document evidencing the interest be registered as soon as possible after receiving the interest in the property. The following example shows what can happen if you don't register your interest right away.

SAMPLE #8
TRANSFER/DEED OF LAND

Province of Ontario

Transfer/Deed of Land
Form 1 — Land Registration Reform Act, 1984

A

FOR OFFICE USE ONLY

(1) Registry [X] Land Titles [ ] (2) Page 1 of 2 pages

(3) Property Identifier(s)   Block   Property   Additional: See Schedule [ ]

(4) Consideration

Fifty One Thousand Nine Hundred...Dollars $51,900.00

(5) Description   This is a: Property Division [ ] Property Consolidation [ ]

Lot 62, Plan 10572, City of Toronto,
Municipality of Metropolitan Toronto

New Property Identifiers   Additional: See Schedule [ ]

Executions   Additional: See Schedule [ ]

(6) This Document Contains   (a) Redescription New Easement Plan/Sketch [ ]   (b) Schedule for: Additional Parties [ ] Description [ ] Other [ ]   (7) Interest/Estate Transferred Fee Simple

(8) Transferor(s) The transferor hereby transfers the land to the transferee and certifies that the transferor is at least eighteen years old and that
Verna Vendor is my spouse

Name(s)	Signature(s)	Date of Signature Y M D
VENDOR, Victor	*Victor Vendor*	1985 06 28

(9) Spouse(s) of Transferor(s) I hereby consent to this transaction

Name(s)	Signature(s)	Date of Signature Y M D
VENDOR, Verna	*Verna Vendor*	1985 06 28

(10) Transferor(s) Address for Service   456 Some Street, Toronto, Ontario, M7Q 8R9

(11) Transferee(s)

	Date of Birth Y M D
PURCHASER, Peter	1959 04 20
PURCHASER, Paula	1962 02 28
joint tenants	

(12) Transferee(s) Address for Service   123 Any Street, Toronto, Ontario, M1N 203

(13) Transferor(s) The transferor verifies that to the best of the transferor's knowledge and belief, this transfer does not contravene section 49 of the Planning Act, 1983.   Date of Signature Y M D   Date of Signature Y M D

Signature.

Solicitor for Transferor(s) I have explained the effect of section 49 of the Planning Act, 1983 to the transferor and I have made inquiries of the transferor to determine that this transfer does not contravene that section and based on the information supplied by the transferor, to the best of my knowledge and belief, this transfer does not contravene that section. I am an Ontario solicitor in good standing.   Date of Signature Y M D

Name and Address of Solicitor   Signature.

(14) Solicitor for Transferee(s) I have investigated the title to this land and to abutting land where relevant and I am satisfied that the title records reveal no contravention as set out in subclause 49 (21a) (c) (ii) of the Planning Act, 1983 and that to the best of my knowledge and belief this transfer does not contravene section 49 of the Planning Act 1983. I act independently of the solicitor for the transferor(s) and I am an Ontario solicitor in good standing.   Date of Signature Y M D

Name and Address of Solicitor   Signature.

Planning Act — OPTIONAL / Affix Statement by Solicitor for Transferee(s) here if necessary

(15) Assessment Roll Number of Property   Cty 06 Mun 35 Map 060 Sub 000 Par 00000

(16) Municipal Address of Property
123 Any Street
Toronto, Ontario
M1N 203

(17) Document Prepared by:
NEVER A. DOUBT
Barrister and Solicitor
4 Courthouse Street
Toronto, Ontario
M2M 2M2

FOR OFFICE USE ONLY

Fees and Tax	
Registration Fee	
Land Transfer Tax	
Total	

10173 (12 84)

127

Form 1 - Land Transfer Tax Act
Affidavit of Residence and of Value of the Consideration
Refer to all instructions on reverse side.

IN THE MATTER OF THE CONVEYANCE OF *(insert brief description of land)* __Lot 62, Plan 10572, Toronto__

BY *(print names of all transferors in full)* __Victor Vendor__

TO *(see instruction 1 and print names of all transferees in full)* __Peter Purchaser and Paula Purchaser__

I, *(see instruction 2 and print name(s) in full)* __Peter Purchaser__

MAKE OATH AND SAY THAT:

1. I am *(place a clear mark within the square opposite that one of the following paragraphs that describes the capacity of the deponent(s)): (see instruction 2)*

   ☐ (a) A person in trust for whom the land conveyed in the above-described conveyance is being conveyed;

   ☐ (b) A trustee named in the above-described conveyance to whom the land is being conveyed;

   ☒ (c) A transferee named in the above-described conveyance;

   ☐ (d) The authorized agent or solicitor acting in this transaction for *(insert name(s) of principal(s))* _____

   _____ described in paragraph(s) (a), (b), (c) above; *(strike out references to inapplicable paragraphs)*

   ☐ (e) The President, Vice-President, Manager, Secretary, Director, or Treasurer authorized to act for *(insert name(s) of corporation(s))* _____

   _____ described in paragraph(s) (a), (b), (c) above; *(strike out references to inapplicable paragraphs)*

   ☐ (f) A transferee described in paragraph( ) *(insert only one of paragraph (a), (b) or (c) above, as applicable)* and am making this affidavit on my own behalf and on behalf of *(insert name of spouse)* _____ who is my spouse described in paragraph ( ) *(insert only one of paragraph (a), (b) or (c) above, as applicable)* and as such, I have personal knowledge of the facts herein deposed to.

2. *(To be completed where the value of the consideration for the conveyance exceeds $250,000).*
   I have read and considered the definition of "single family residence" set out in clause 1(1)(ja) of the Act. The land conveyed in the above-described conveyance

   ☐ contains at least one and not more than two single family residences.

   ☐ does not contain a single family residence.

   ☐ contains more than two single family residences. *(see instruction 3)*

   Note: Clause 2(1) (d) imposes an additional tax at the rate of one-half of one per cent upon the value of consideration in excess of $250,000 where the conveyance contains at least one and not more than two single family residences.

3. I have read and considered the definitions of "non-resident corporation" and "non-resident person" set out respectively in clauses 1(1)(f) and (g) of the Act and each of the following persons to whom or in trust for whom the land is being conveyed in the above-described conveyance is a "non-resident corporation" or a "non-resident person" as set out in the Act *(see instructions 4 and 5)*

   __none__

4. **THE TOTAL CONSIDERATION FOR THIS TRANSACTION IS ALLOCATED AS FOLLOWS:**

   (a) Monies paid or to be paid in cash .... $ __20,737.10__

   (b) Mortgages. (i) Assumed *(show principal and interest to be credited against purchase price)* ... $ __24,962.90__

   (ii) Given back to vendor .... $ __6,200.00__

   (c) Property transferred in exchange *(detail below)* .... $ __NIL__

   (d) Securities transferred to the value of *(detail below)* .... $ __NIL__

   (e) Liens, legacies, annuities and maintenance charges to which transfer is subject ... $ __NIL__

   (f) Other valuable consideration subject to land transfer tax *(detail below)* .... $ __NIL__

   (g) VALUE OF LAND, BUILDING, FIXTURES AND GOODWILL SUBJECT TO LAND TRANSFER TAX *(Total of (a) to (f))* ... $ __51,900.00__ $ __51,900.00__

   (h) VALUE OF ALL CHATTELS - items of tangible personal property *(Retail Sales Tax is payable on the value of all chattels unless exempt under the provisions of the "Retail Sales Tax Act", R.S.O. 1980, c 454, as amended)* ... $ __1,000.00__

   (i) Other consideration for transaction not included in (g) or (h) above .... $ __NIL__

   (j) TOTAL CONSIDERATION .... $ __52,900.00__

   All Blanks Must Be Filled In. Insert "Nil" Where Applicable

5. If consideration is nominal, describe relationship between transferor and transferee and state purpose of conveyance. *(see instruction 6)* __not applicable__

6. If the consideration is nominal, is the land subject to any encumbrance? __not applicable__

7. Other remarks and explanations, if necessary. _____

Sworn before me at the __City of Toronto__
in the __Municipality of Metropolitan Toronto__
this __29__ day of __June__ 19 __85__

A Commissioner for taking Affidavits, etc.

Peter Purchaser *(signature(s))*
Peter Purchaser

Property Information Record

A. Describe nature of instrument _____

B. (i) Address of property being conveyed *(if available)* _____

   (ii) Assessment Roll No *(if available)* _____

C. Mailing address(es) for future Notices of Assessment under the Assessment Act for property being conveyed *(see instruction 7)* _____

D. (i) Registration number for last conveyance of property being conveyed *(if available)* _____

   (ii) Legal description of property conveyed. Same as in D (i) above   Yes ☐   No ☐   Not known ☐

E. Name(s) and address(es) of each transferee's solicitor _____

	For Land Registry Office use only
	REGISTRATION NO
	Land Registry Office No.
	Registration Date

SAMPLE #8 — Continued

Instructions

1. Where any transferee (other than a joint tenant) is taking less than the whole interest in the property being acquired, then the percentage ownership of each such transferee must be clearly indicated beside his/her respective name.

2. (i) It should be noted that if all *deponents* are not entitled to mark the same square in paragraph 1 of the Affidavit, then more than one Affidavit will be required. Only those deponents who are entitled to mark the same square in paragraph 1 may swear the same Affidavit.

   (ii) This Affidavit is required to be made by each transferee named in the conveyance, by each person in trust for whom the land conveyed in the conveyance described is being conveyed and by each trustee named in the conveyance to whom the land is conveyed.

   (iii) However, any of the transferees may have the Affidavit made on his behalf by an agent authorized in writing to make the Affidavit or by his solicitor. (See clause (d) of paragraph 1 of Affidavit.)

   (iv) The Affidavit for a transferee that is a corporation may be made by its President, Vice-President, Manager, Secretary, Director or Treasurer. (See clause (e) of paragraph 1 of Affidavit.)

   (v) Where transferees are married to each other, either spouse may make the Affidavit on behalf of him/herself and the other. (See clause (f) of paragraph 1 of Affidavit.)

3. Extract of clause 1(1)(ja) of the Act:

   (ja) "single family residence" means,

   (i) a unit or proposed unit under the Condominium Act, or

   (ii) a structure or part of a structure,

   that is designed for occupation as the residence of one family, including dependants or domestic employees of a member of the family, whether or not rent is paid for the occupation of any part of such residence, and whether or not the land on which the residence is situated is zoned for residential use, and "single family residence" includes any such residence that is to be constructed as part of the arrangement relating to a conveyance of land, but does not include any such residence constructed or to be constructed on agricultural land where the transferor with respect to the land conveyed meets the eligibility requirements for a farm tax reduction rebate contained in clause 4(b) or (c) of Ontario Regulation 716/83 made under the Ministry of Agriculture and Food Act.

4. Note: Subsection 1(3) provides, inter alia, that an individual shall be considered to be "ordinarily resident in Canada" if, at the time the expression is being applied, he has sojourned in Canada during the next preceding twenty-four months for a period of, or periods the aggregate of which is 366 days or more.

   Extract of clauses 1(1)(f) and (g) of the Act:

   (f) "non-resident corporation" means a corporation incorporated, formed or otherwise organized in Canada or elsewhere,

   (i) that has allotted and issued shares to which are attached 50 per cent or more of the voting rights ordinarily exercisable at meetings of the shareholders of the corporation and that are owned by one or more non resident persons, but this subclause does not apply where it is established to the satisfaction of the Minister that such one or more non-resident persons do not in fact directly or indirectly exercise control over the corporation and that subclause (v) does not apply to the corporation,

   (ii) that has allotted and issued shares to which are attached 25 per cent or more of the voting rights ordinarily exercisable at meetings of the shareholders of the corporation and that are owned by any one non-resident person or by that person and one or more persons who are associates of that person and who are themselves non-resident persons, but this subclause does not apply where it is established to the satisfaction of the Minister that such non-resident person does not in fact directly or indirectly exercise control over

the corporation and that subclause (v) does not apply to the corporation,

   (iii) one-half or more of the directors of which, or of the persons occupying the position of director by whatever name called, are individuals who are non-resident persons,

   (iv) without share capital and one-half or more of the members of which are non-resident persons,

   (v) that is controlled directly or indirectly by one or more non-resident persons, including a non-resident corporation within the definition contained in the provisions of this clause other than this subclause,

   (vi) one-quarter or more of the paid-up capital of which is held by a non-resident person or by that person and one or more persons who are associates of that person and who are themselves non-resident persons,

   (vii) one-half or more of the paid-up capital of which is held by one or more non-resident persons,

   (viii) that would be required on dissolving, winding up, or any other distribution that is not a dividend, to distribute one-quarter or more of its surplus to a non-resident person or to that person and one or more persons who are associates of that person and who are themselves non-resident persons, or

   (ix) that would be required on dissolving, winding-up, or any other distribution of surplus that is not a dividend, to distribute one-half or more of its surplus to one or more non-resident persons."

   (g) "non-resident person" means,

   (i) an individual who is not ordinarily resident in Canada or who, if ordinarily resident in Canada, is neither a Canadian citizen nor an individual who has been lawfully admitted to Canada for permanent residence in Canada,

   (ii) a partnership, syndicate, association or other organization of whatsoever kind of which one-half or more of the members are non-resident persons within the meaning of subclause (i), (iii) or (iv) or in which interests representing in value 50 per cent or more of the total value of the property of such partnership, syndicate, association or other organization are beneficially owned by non-resident persons within the meaning of subclause (i), (iii) or (iv),

   (iii) a trust in which non-resident persons within the meaning of subclause (i), (iii) or (iv) have 50 per cent or more of the beneficial interests in the corpus of the trust or in the income arising therefrom, and "trust" includes the trustees under such a trust in their capacity as the trustees thereof, or

   (iv) a non-resident corporation.

5. Insert the name and place of residence - or in the case of a corporation, the place of incorporation - of any transferee who is a non-resident person. If space is insufficient, attach a list of those transferees who are non-resident persons. If none of the transferees is non-resident, insert 'none'.

   Note: Where the person named in the instrument as grantee is taking title on behalf of another person(s), the residency status to be recited must be that of the person or persons who are the beneficial owners of the land - not that of the grantee named in the instrument. This applies regardless of whether the trustee or nominee capacity of the grantee named in the instrument is indicated on the instrument.

6. Explain purpose of transfer: natural love and affection, pursuant to court order, separation agreement, etc.

7. Insert mailing address(es) where municipal assessment notices for property being conveyed are to be forwarded after closing of this transaction.

NOTE: IN ADDITION TO ATTACHING THIS AFFIDAVIT TO THE CONVEYANCE TENDERED FOR REGISTRATION, ONE UNATTACHED, COMPLETED COPY MUST BE TENDERED TO THE LAND REGISTRAR AT THE TIME OF REGISTRATION.

129

Penny McScrooge buys her property from "Fast" Eddie O'Greedy. Eddie provides Penny with a deed or transfer and Penny pays the purchase price. Penny leaves her deed for a couple of days before taking it down to the Land Registry Office and "Fast" Eddie, who is not an honest man, sells his property again to Johnny Kumlately, who registers his document immediately. To Penny's horror, when she goes to register she will find that Johnny Kumlately is recognized as having a legitimate interest in the property. Her only right of action will be to sue "Fast" Eddie for damages for fraud.

A search of title will normally be done twice. The first time will be when the search of title is made and the second time will be when the title is registered. This latter search is merely an updating of the previous search of title to the time of closing and is commonly known as a "subsearch."

A search of the title to land registered under the Registry Act system must cover the period of 40 years prior to the transaction plus whatever time is necessary prior to this 40-year period to obtain a clear title.

The word "conveyance" is used throughout this book to mean a transfer of the ownership of land. For example, if a house has been sold in 1912, 1940, 1958, 1979 and if the search must be made up to and including a date in 1985, the title must be searched for the 40 years prior to 1985 and then to the first clear conveyance, which would be in 1912.

This is the beginning point of the search and the searcher must make an examination of the 1912 sale of the property to make sure that it is a clear conveyance of the land. In addition, the searcher must examine all subsequent dealings with the land in order to ascertain that they have been properly made and, accordingly, that the vendor has the title that he or she claims to have in the agreement of purchase and sale.

The term "chain of title" is often used to describe the history of the ownership or dealings with real estate and in the above example, the chain of title would have four links. Your lawyer would examine all of the links in the chain of title to make sure that the links are complete and that the chain is properly joined.

In the Land Titles Act system, the title to the real estate is stated as a fact by an official called the Land Registrar. A search of land registered under the land titles system consists of viewing the abstract of the title in order to ascertain who is the owner of the property and what encumbrances, restrictions or charges are outstanding against the title.

Referring again to the analogy of the chain of title, in the land titles system, one is not required to inspect the entire chain of title but only the last link in the chain as well as any other links of encumbrances that are outstanding.

Thus, in the Land Titles Act system, the Land Registrar assumes the responsibility for stating whether the chain of title is sufficient and proper, and this responsibility is insured by a fund established under the Land Titles Act. If the Land Registrar makes a mistake in evaluation of the chain of title, a claim may be made against this insurance fund. However, the insurance fund does not provide protection against things which are beyond the control of the Land Registrar, such as fraud and forgery.

In Ontario, the number of claims made against this insurance fund has been very small and the credit for this fact must be given to the quality of the people who occupy the position of the various Land Registrars.

When you tender a document for registration in the Land Titles Office the document is thoroughly checked by a land titles official who ascertains that the document does what it purports to do and has been sufficiently well executed. Contrast this with the Registry Act system, where the responsibility for ascertaining the condition of the title is on the person who searches the title.

At this point, you may well wonder why all the land in Ontario is not registered under the Land Titles Act system. There are basically two reasons.

(a) The Land Titles Act system does not operate in all areas of Ontario.

(b) In order to bring a title under the Land Titles Act system, an application must be made to the Land Registrar and this application can be costly.

As a result of legislative changes, the Land Titles Act system (if this system has been invoked in the locality in which the land is situated) is required to be used for newly developed plans of subdivision and condominium plans. Accordingly, this requirement will create the result, as time goes on, of having more properties governed by the Land Titles Act system and fewer governed by the Registry Act system.

4. Searches under a subdivision agreement

As previously mentioned, the title to many residential properties is subject to the provisions of a subdivision agreement. The subdivision agreement is a contract between the owner of land and the municipality in which the land is located where the owner of the land usually pledges the land as security for the performance of its obligations under the subdivision agreement.

The subdivision agreement will contain various obligations that must be complied with by the owner of the land and, if the owner of the land does not comply with these obligations, certain prohibitions, such as a prohibition of occupancy of the land, may be imposed.

Most subdivision agreements require that the obligations of the owner of the land are subject to the approval of various municipal officials and, accordingly, it will be necessary for the purchaser, through his or her lawyer, to ascertain from the requisite municipal officials whether the various provisions of the subdivision agreement have been complied with to the satisfaction of that municipal official.

5. Condominium searches

In addition to the usual searches in a purchase of residential real estate, there are additional searches that must be made if it is the purchase of a condominium.

The search of title will indicate that there are documents (the declaration, the description and the by-laws) that must be registered under the Condominium Act. These documents must be searched to make sure that there are no unreasonable restrictions in these documents regarding the activities of an owner.

Also, a condominium purchaser will wish to be advised about some or all of the following matters relating to the condominium project:

(a) Whether there are any reserve funds or contingency funds

(b) The amount of money that must be contributed to the contingency fund or the reserve fund

(c) The amount of common expense

(d) Whether all other unit owners are in good standing with respect to their payment of common expenses and contributions to the reserve fund and contingency fund

(e) Whether the condominium corporation is involved in any litigation

(f) Whether there have been any meetings held or called for the purpose of either terminating the condominium government or amending the declaration and by-laws.

Of course, there may be several other matters that the prospective purchaser may wish to know about the condominium project. (Please refer to the section on purchasing a condominium.)

The Condominium Act now provides a mechanism for a purchaser to receive much of this information, as well as some protection for the purchaser if this information is not provided. The proposed purchaser of a condominium unit or his or her solicitor can request at his or her expense (usually $25) a certificate from the Condominium Corporation confirming such information and details as are required by the Condominium Act. This certificate is commonly called an "estoppel certificate" and an example is shown in Sample #9. In addition to this certificate, the Condominium Corporation is required to provide to the purchaser a copy of each of the following:

(a) the last annual financial statements of the corporation,

(b) the corporation's current budget,

(c) the declaration,

(d) the corporation's by-laws,

(e) the corporation's rules,

(f) the corporation's management agreement, and

(g) all current insurance certificates.

If the Condominium Corporation does not provide this certificate within eight days after it receives a request for it, the Condominium Corporation is deemed, as against the person requesting the certificate, to have given a certificate stating no default. In other words, the Condominium Corporation is prohibited from making a claim against the requesting party for any matters that would have been shown as outstanding in the certificate if it had been issued in a timely manner. Some Condominium Corporations will provide more information than the minimum requirements set forth in the Condominium Act. Sample #9 shows only the minimum requirements.

6. Problems encountered in the search

Once the search of title has been prepared, it will be examined and compared with the title claimed by the vendor in the agreement of purchase and sale. In addition to looking for outstanding charges and encumbrances, such as mortgages or liens, your lawyer will look for other matters affecting the title to the property being purchased. Some of the most common matters encountered in current real estate conveyancing follow.

Many of the titles to residential real estate are subject to an easement in favor of the local municipality, hydro electric commission or supplier of telephone services. These easements are usually located along the rear or the side boundary of the property and usually are four to eight feet in width. The purpose of these easements is to allow the municipality, the hydro electric commission or telephone company to enter the property and install their lines of service and, subsequently, to repair, operate and maintain these lines of service.

The standard form of this type of easement usually contains a covenant by the interested party to repair or restore the surface of the land if the land must be disturbed. However, you cannot build on the easement and, in fact, must keep the easement relatively clear of obstructions.

Many older homes do not contain a driveway wholly on the property, but rather, contain a driveway that is shared with the owner of the neighboring property. This driveway is commonly called a "mutual driveway." A mutual driveway is formed by neighbors granting to each other a common right of way over a specific portion of their property.

Like an easement, a right of way cannot be built upon or impeded with to the detriment of the other party involved unless the agreement creating the right of way specifically so provides.

Another common matter arising from the search of title is the matter of a restrictive covenant. A restrictive covenant is a promise by a land owner to an owner of other land that the former owner will not do certain things with his or her property.

A restrictive covenant may, by its terms, be binding upon subsequent purchasers of the land. For example, a common form of restrictive covenant in current use is that the plans and specifications of any building to be built on the land must receive the approval of the subdivider of the land. This type of restrictive covenant attempts to ensure that a certain quality of housing will be maintained in the specified area.

The law surrounding restrictive covenants is very complex and technical; if you have a problem in this area, legal assistance will be necessary.

Another problem that commonly arises out of the search of title is the problem of dower. (The Family Law Reform Act abolished dower rights after March 31, 1978, but they are still an issue in title searches.) Dower is a right in land in favor of the wife of an owner of land. Dower is an ancient right originally developed in England in order to prevent a husband from leaving his wife penniless on his death.

SAMPLE #9
ESTOPPEL CERTIFICATE

Form 18
Condominium Act
CERTIFICATE

(under subsection 32(8) of the Condominium Act)

Name of Condominium Corporation:
Metropolitan Toronto Condominium
Corporation No. 0000

Current Mailing Address:
123 Any Street, Management Office,
Toronto, Ontario, M1M 1M1

Current Address for Service:
123 Any Street, Management Office,
Toronto, Ontario, M1M 1M1

Metropolitan Toronto Condominium Corporation No. 0000 (hereinafter referred to as the "Corporation")

The Corporation hereby certifies that as of the date hereof:

1. The owner of unit 12345, level 206 (suite 2060, 123 Any Street, Toronto, Ontario, M1M 1M1) of Metropolitan Toronto Condominium Plan No. 0000, registered in the Land Registry Office for the Land Titles Division of Metropolitan Toronto, is not in default in the payment of common expenses;

2. The amount of $1 948.56 in prepaid common expenses stands to the credit of the said owner in the Corporation's record;

3. A payment on account of common expenses of $325.00 is due on July 1, 1987 for the period July 1, 1987 to July 31, 1987;

4. The current budget, a copy of which is attached hereto, is accurate and may result in a deficit of $1 000.00;

5. The corporation's reserve funds amounts to $52 426.87 as of June 1, 1987;

6. The Corporation has no knowledge of any circumstances that may result in an increase in the common expenses for the said unit;

7. The Corporation is not presently a party to any legal action;

8. The Corporation is not presently considering any substantial addition, alteration or improvement to or renovation of the common elements or any substantial change in the assets of the corporation;

9. The Corporation has secured all policies of insurance that are required under the provisions of the Condominium Act;

10. The property manager is Ace Management Corp., 123 Any Street, Management Office, Toronto, Ontario, M1M 1M1, (416-666-6666);

11. The Directors and Officers of the Corporation are as follows:

Name	Address	Position
John Q. President	123 Any Street, Apt. 1, Toronto, Ontario, M1M 1M1	President
John Q. Secretary	123 Any Street, Apt. 2, Toronto, Ontario, M1M 1M1	Secretary
John Q. Treasurer	123 Any Street, Apt. 3, Toronto, Ontario, M1M 1M1	Treasurer

Dated at Toronto this 8th day of June, 1987.

Metropolitan Toronto Condominium Corporation No. 0000

Per: _____
                              President
                                                          c/s

Per: _____

Pursuant to the provisions of the Act and the Regulations the Corporation may charge a fee not to exceed $25.00 for this Certificate and the accompanying statements and information.

This Certificate shall be accompanied by the following statements and information.

1. A copy of the last annual financial statements of the corporation, audited if available.

2. A copy of the corporation's current budget.

3. A copy of the corporation's declaration.

4. A copy of the corporation's by-laws.

5. A copy of the corporation's rules.

6. A copy of any management agreement.

7. A copy of all current insurance certificates.

Many problems arising out of the search of title are related to the conveyancing of the land from the estate of a deceased owner. Another common problem arising out of the search of title, particularly when the land is registered under the Registry Act system, is the problem of a sale of the property for arrears of realty taxes or mortgage payments. This problem was prevalent in the depression years of the 1930s and appears on many searches of title as one of the links. In order to transfer property for default of taxes or mortgage payments, the law now and in 1930 requires that certain detailed procedures be taken in order to properly convey the title. When a matter such as this arises on a search of title, your lawyer must determine that all of the necessary procedures have been taken in order to properly convey the title.

The Planning Act has made it necessary to search the title to adjacent property to the premises being purchased as well as the title to the premises being purchased. This matter is further discussed on page 143.

The above matters are some of the more common problems to arise out of the search of title. A complete discussion of these matters and any other problems that may arise on the search of title is beyond the scope of this book. In any event, these are all matters which should be handled by your lawyer.

7. Requisitions

A requisition was briefly mentioned earlier. Simply, it is some requirement that the purchaser demands to be satisfied before completion. What the purchaser can demand is dictated by the agreement of purchase and sale. There are two types of requisitions. First, there are requisitions as to the state of the vendor's title and, secondly, requisitions as to the conveyance, which arise out of the offer or agreement of purchase and sale itself.

An example of a requisition regarding the title is when there is an outstanding encumbrance registered against the title which the purchaser requires the vendor to discharge prior to closing date.

In this type of requisition, the purchaser is complaining that the state of the vendor's title is not as described in the offer or agreement and the requisition of the purchaser is a demand that the matter be attended to.

An example of a requisition regarding the conveyance is the requirement that the vendor provide on closing a statutory declaration regarding section 116 of the Income Tax Act. This type of requisition can only be made and need only be complied with if the subject matter of the requisition is contained in the offer or agreement of purchase and sale. In other words, this type of requisition must be included in the offer or agreement or else the vendor is not required to provide it.

To protect the purchaser, the standard form agreement of purchase and sale contains a provision that the purchaser is to be allowed a specified number of days to examine the title at his or her own expense. This will be the time in which requisitions as to title must be made.

To protect yourself, you should fill in this blank with a substantial number of days, at least 30, in order to allow your lawyer ample time to make the search and consider the state of the title.

There are certain requisitions common to every conveyance. These are as follows:

(a) The statement of adjustments, a document containing the accounting of all matters between the vendor and purchaser

(b) A draft of the deed to be provided on closing by the vendor's lawyer and checked over by the purchaser's lawyer

(c) A sketch of survey if the vendor has a sketch of survey

(d) Declaration of possession

(e) Evidence of compliance with section 116 of the Income Tax Act (As mentioned, there is some doubt as to whether this is an item that the purchaser is allowed to requisition if it is not contained in the offer or agreement of purchase and sale. At any rate, most purchasers will submit this requisition and most vendors are willing to comply with this requisition in order that the closing of the transaction is not jeopardized. Most forms of agreement of purchase and sale now make this a matter of conveyance.)

(f) Proof from the vendor that the vendor has made all of the payments for which compensation is claimed on the statement of adjustments

In addition to these requisitions, the purchaser will submit as requisition to the particular conveyance, any other matters contained in the offer or agreement of purchase and sale that place an obligation on the vendor to be complied with prior to the closing of the transaction.

8. Statutory liens (a claim against the title to property contained in an act of the provincial or federal government)

Many statutes or laws contain a provision that the failure to comply with certain sections of the statute will result in a lien being placed on real estate of the person who is liable.

This is done in order to make it easier for the government to enforce a statute. Practically this imposes an obligation upon both the vendor and the purchaser. In other words, by placing a lien on the property, the statute imposes an obligation on the purchaser to ascertain if a lien exists and on the vendor to comply with the provisions of the statute. Some examples of statutory liens are as follows:

(a) Realty tax lien

If an owner of real estate does not pay the required amount of realty taxes, the municipality in which the land is located will have a lien to the extent of the unpaid realty taxes, together with interest and penalties. The lawyer for the purchaser will usually obtain a tax certificate from the treasurer of the municipality certifying either that realty taxes have been paid up until a certain date or that arrears are outstanding as of a certain date. Where appropriate it would also show if any part of the lands have been sold for arrears of taxes and whether a certificate of tax arrears has been registered against the title within 18 months previous to the date of the certificate. The usual cost of the tax certificates is between $3 and $10.

(b) Corporation Tax Act

The Corporation Tax Act imposes a lien on all property of a corporation for arrears of corporation tax, interest and penalties and for failure to file the requisite information. This lien must be registered on the title to the property.

(c) Retail Sales Tax Act

The Retail Sales Tax Act imposes a lien against the property of anyone who is in arrears of payment of retail sales tax.

(d) Writs of execution

A writ of execution is a document filed with the sheriff of a county or district stating that a judgment has been obtained in a court whereby a person (judgment debtor) is indebted to another person (judgment creditor) as a result of a legal proceeding. A writ of execution imposes a lien against the property of the judgment debtor which effectively bars the owner from selling or in any way dealing with the property without first paying the judgment. Thus, a purchaser, through a lawyer, should make a search for any writs of execution and this search must be made against the name of the vendor and any other people who have owned the property during the time of the chain of title. For land under the Registry Act system, this search is usually made by obtaining a Sheriff's Certificate and, if the Sheriff's Certificate indicates that there are writs outstanding, the vendor has the responsibility of correcting the situation.

For land under the Land Titles Act system, this search must be made with the Land Registrar, and the vendor's obligation is the same.

(e) Workers' Compensation Act

The Workers' Compensation Act provides a lien against the property of persons who have not made the necessary contributions under the Workers' Compensation Act. A lien claimant must be registered in the same manner as a writ of execution in order to bind the property. Thus, a search for writs of execution will also indicate whether there is a lien claimed against the property under this act.

9. Section 49 of the Planning Act

As already mentioned, the Planning Act imposes a certain amount of government control on the development of real estate. This act, and in particular, section 49, restricts the subdivision of larger units of land into smaller units. In order to register a plan of subdivision, one must obtain the requisite municipal approvals.

More specifically, section 49 of the Planning Act includes provisions that no person may convey or mortgage land unless one of the following situations exists:

(a) The land being conveyed is the whole of a lot or block on a registered plan of subdivision.

(b) The person conveying or mortgaging the land does not retain an ownership interest in any land abutting the land that is being conveyed or mortgaged.

(c) The land is being conveyed to the government of Canada, Ontario or the municipality, district or county.

(d) The land is being conveyed for the construction of a transmission line, as defined in the Ontario Energy Board Act.

(e) A consent is obtained from the local Committee of Adjustment, Land Division Committee or the Minister of Municipal Affairs.

If a conveyance or mortgage is made contrary to section 49, it will fail to create any interest in the land in favor of the person to whom it was conveyed or mortgaged. Thus, like several of the other statutes that have been previously discussed, the Planning Act puts the obligation of compliance upon both the vendor and purchaser of the property. For this reason, the purchaser must search the title of the property abutting the land that he or she is purchasing in order to ascertain that none of this neighboring property is owned by the vendor. This search must be made back to 1967.

If a purchaser is purchasing the whole of a lot on a registered plan of subdivision or if the purchaser is purchasing all of the land owned by the vendor (in other words, the vendor does not own any neighboring land), there will be no contravention of section 49.

If it is necessary to make an application to the municipal authorities, it must be shown that the subdivision of the land is proper and in accordance with current land development standards. This consent is commonly called a consent to "severance" and if obtained, the consent will either be contained in a decision of the Committee of Adjustment or in an endorsement on the deed, transfer or mortgage signed by the relevant officials. The consent should be registered on the title. There is an additional exception provided in the Planning Act for a conveyance of part of a lot on a registered plan of subdivision and that is where the council of a municipality may pass a by-law providing that section 49(5) does not apply to land that is within such registered plan or plans of subdivision. This by-law must be approved by the Minister of Municipal Affairs.

10. Declaration of possession

A declaration of possession is a statutory declaration, sworn under oath, whereby the vendor swears that certain matters pertaining to the property have been true during the period of ownership. The purpose of the declaration of possession is to confirm various matters that are not described in the documents comprising the chain of title.

It is common conveyancing practice that the declaration of possession is prepared by the purchaser's lawyer and forwarded to the vendor's lawyer who will review its contents with the vendor and have it verified by the vendor. There are standard forms in common use. Many lawyers will start with a standard form of one type or another and add to or delete from it, as the particular conveyance may require. An example of the standard form of declaration of possession is shown in Sample #10.

SAMPLE #10
DECLARATION OF POSSESSION

Declaration of Possession

Dye & Durham Co. Limited 76 Richmond Street East, Toronto
Form No. 129

DOMINION OF CANADA
PROVINCE OF ONTARIO
JUDICIAL DISTRICT OF
YORK

IN THE MATTER OF THE TITLE

to No. 1234 ANY   Street, being
in the City of Toronto, in the
Municipality of Metropolitan Toronto

AND THE SALE THEREOF

FROM   VICTOR VENDOR

To Wit:

I, VICTOR VENDOR
of the   City   of   Toronto
of Metropolitan Toronto,

To   PETER PURCHASER and PAULA PURCHASER
in the Municipality

Do Solemnly Declare:

1. That subject to a mortgage in favor of The Life Insurance Company
and
on which there is due for principal $24,851.17 interest from the   20th day of   June,   19 85
and to one in favor of ------------------------------------ upon which there is owing for
principal $ ---------, and interest from the -------- day of -------------- 19-- ,
I am the absolute owner of the above mentioned lands and either personally or by my tenants have been
in the actual, peaceable, continuous, exclusive, open, undisturbed and undisputed possession and occupation
thereof, and of the houses and other buildings used in connection therewith since on or about the   15th
day of   June,   1962   when I obtained a conveyance thereof.

2. That save and except the above mentioned mortgage and any taxes and local improvement rates
charged thereon there is no encumbrance or easement whatsoever affecting the said lands.

3. That I am not aware of any person or persons or corporations having any claim or interest in the
said lands or any part thereof adverse to or inconsistent with my title and I am positive that none such
exists.

4. That my possession and occupation of the above mentioned lands have been undisturbed throughout
by any action, suit or other proceedings or adverse possession or otherwise on the part of any person
whomsoever and during such possession and occupation no payment has ever been made or acknowledgment
of title given by me, or, so far as I know, by anyone else, to any person in respect of any right, title, interest
or claim upon the said lands.

5. That the deeds, evidences of title and other papers which have been produced by me are all the
title deeds, evidences of title and other papers relating to the title to the said lands that are in my possession
or power and that to the best of my knowledge and belief the said title deeds and papers produced and this
declaration and the registered title fully and fairly disclose all facts material to the title claimed by me and
all contracts and dealings which affect the same or any part thereof so far as I have any knowledge thereof.

6. That to the best of my knowledge and belief the buildings used in connection with the premises are
situate wholly within the limits of the lands above described, and there is no dispute as to the boundaries of
the said lands and that the same during the time I have been the owner thereof have been completely
fenced. I have never heard of any claim of easement affecting the lands, either for light, drainage, or right
of way or otherwise.

7. That a portion of the said lands and premises are occupied by
Tom Tenant, as tenant on a month to month tenancy and the said
tenant has no right to purchase the said lands.

8. That there are no mechanics' liens registered against the said lands nor any claims for which such
liens could be registered as all such have been paid in full.

9. That   Verna Vendor   who has executed the
said conveyance together with myself is my wife and we are both over the age of   eighteen years.

10. There are no executions in the Sheriff's hands affecting the said lands to my knowledge.

11. All taxes on the said lands have been paid up to the   31st   day of   December   19 85

AND I make this solemn declaration conscientiously believing it to be true and knowing that it is of
the same force and effect as if made under oath and by virtue of "The Canada Evidence Act".

DECLARED before me at the   City
of   Toronto
in the   Municipality
of   Metropolitan Toronto
this   28th
day of   June   19 85,
(signed) *I.C. You*
A Commissioner, Etc.

(signed)   *Victor Vendor*

145

11. Discharging previous mortgages

It is a common practice for the vendor to be required to discharge a pre-existing mortgage arising out of his or her arrangements with the purchaser. In strict legal doctrine, when the vendor is responsible for removing a mortgage, the purchaser is entitled to insist on the mortgage being released from the title on or before closing and a vendor cannot legally require a purchaser to complete a real estate transaction unless such a mortgage is released.

If a purchaser wishes to insist on this legal right, a problem is created for the vendor where the vendor requires a portion of the purchase price to be paid to satisfy the pre-existing mortgage account. This problem is usually resolved in one of the following ways.

(a) The vendor arranges to have a discharge of mortgage prepared and available for the closing and directs the purchaser to pay the pre-existing mortgagee the balance of that account. This is the most satisfactory arrangement because the purchaser, on closing, receives title to the property, free of the mortgage. However, many mortgagees, particularly most institutional lenders, will refuse to do this.

(b) The vendor and purchaser make an agreement on closing date that the transaction be completed despite the existence of the mortgage encumbrance, on the promise of the vendor's lawyer to obtain and register a discharge of the mortgage encumbrance after the closing of the transaction and, if a discharge of mortgage cannot be obtained, on the promise of the vendor's lawyer to take such legal proceeding as may be required.

Although both these methods are common due to the predominance of institutional lenders in the residential real estate market, the second alternative is used more frequently.

It is important for the purchaser to realize there is an element of risk between the time of closing and the time of registration of the discharge of the pre-existing mortgage.

Unfortunately, there does not seem to be any way of reducing this risk short of requiring the vendor to come up with money independently to clear off the mortgage. In many cases, this would have the effect of preventing the transaction from going through.

12. Mortgage to be assumed

If a purchaser is taking over the vendor's mortgage, he or she will want the following information from the mortgagee (lender):

(a) The balance owing under the mortgage at the date of closing

(b) The terms of the mortgage, such as the rate of interest, the amount of the instalments required, the date upon which instalments are to be paid and the privileges in favor of the mortgagor that may be exercised by the purchaser

(c) That the mortgage has not been altered, amended or modified in any way

(d) That there are no outstanding matters between the vendor and the mortgagee which would be detrimental to the purchaser's assumption of the mortgage

It is common for the vendor's lawyer to obtain a mortgage statement from the mortgagee and to give this mortgage statement to the purchaser on closing. (See Sample #11.)

13. The mortgage back

If the vendor is taking a mortgage back from the purchaser, the standard procedure is to have the purchaser's lawyer prepare this. In this situation, the purchaser's lawyer will usually prepare a standard form of mortgage in accordance with the terms described in the offer or agreement of purchase and sale and forward a draft to the vendor's lawyer for approval.

14. Estate conveyancing

Both in the search of the title and in the completion of the transaction, a conveyance by an estate is probably the most

TO: PETER PURCHASER AND PAULA PURCHASER

AND TO: BARRISTER AND SOLICITOR,
THEIR SOLICITORS

RE: FIRST MORTGAGE, 1234 ANY STREET,
TORONTO, ONTARIO

MORTGAGE STATEMENT

The undersigned, being the first mortgagee under the first mortgage on 1234 Any Street, Toronto, hereby certifies the following with respect to the said first mortgage:

Balance of principal outstanding as of June 20, 1985	$24 851.17
Interest rate — 9½%	
Interest on outstanding principal accruing to June 30, 1985	111.73
Monthly payment required	362.48

Payment dates — 20th day of each and every month in each and every year from and including the 20th day of July, 1985 to and including the 20th day of October, 1990

Maturity date — October 20th, 1990

Privileges — none

DATED at Toronto, this 15th day of May, 198-.

THE LIFE INSURANCE COMPANY

PER:(signed) *Mort Manager*

Mortgage Manager

difficult type of real estate transaction in Ontario. The reason for the difficulty is that there is a mixture of three areas of the law — real estate law, estate law and death taxation law. A brief description of the pitfalls to be avoided in a conveyance by the estate of a deceased person can be summarized as follows:

(a) Proof of death

The realty will be registered in the name of the deceased and, in order to obtain a clear title, a purchaser will wish to have registered on the title to the property confirmation that the deceased person is, in fact, dead. This confirmation is usually provided by an affidavit of a close relative of the deceased person or a death certificate.

(b) Proper appointment of the personal representative

When the identity of the personal representative is determined, he or she can be registered on the title.

(c) Power to convey

The personal representative does not automatically have the right to convey the real estate. This power to convey must be conferred upon the personal representative and this is usually done either by the will or by statute. The purchaser will, or course, require that evidence of the power to convey be registered on the title to the property.

(d) Release of estate claims

In many wills, the deceased will have provided for certain gifts or dispositions. These "gifts" may be a charge upon the real estate until they are paid. In addition, in many estate situations, the payment of the debts of the deceased land owner, including funeral expenses, are a first charge against the real estate. A purchaser will want satisfactory evidence that these claims have, in fact, been paid.

(e) Succession duties

If the deceased died during the time that an act was in force requiring the payment of succession duties arising immediately upon the death of the deceased and requiring that a consent of the requisite government official be obtained in order to convey the property of the deceased, free and clear of this lien, the purchaser will, of course, require that the requisite consent is registered.

15. Statement of adjustments

The statement of adjustments is the document recording the accounting between the vendor and purchaser of all of the matters relevant to the real estate transaction. The statement of adjustments is usually prepared by the vendor's lawyer and a copy is provided to the purchaser's lawyer who checks it for accuracy.

For your information, an example of a statement of adjustments is shown in Sample #12.

In analysing a statement of adjustments, it must be remembered that the vendor is responsible for the payment of all matters relating to the property up to the date of closing and, of course, the purchaser is responsible for all matters and charges after the date of closing.

Thus, if you are a purchaser, the statement of adjustments will credit you with any expenses that you will be paying that are the responsibility of the vendor until the closing and will credit the vendor with any expenditure that has been prepaid by the vendor that is your responsibility. For example, in the insurance adjustment contained in Sample #12 the vendor has paid the insurance premium of $150 relating to the period from June 30, 1984, to June 30, 1987. Since the vendor is only responsible for the payment of this premium from June 30, 1984 to June 30, 1985, the statement of adjustments shows the vendor a credit in the sum of $100.

The statement of adjustments usually contains two columns, the right-hand column being the amounts or items which are allowed to the vendor and the left-hand column being the items or amounts allowed to the purchaser.

On or before closing, the purchaser's lawyer will try to obtain confirmation that all items have, in fact, been paid by the vendor.

16. Is the property being rented?

If all or part of the property sold is being rented, the following matters should be checked.

(a) In order for the tenancy to be permitted, the home should be zoned under the relevant by-law to allow renting, or at least there should be no legal impediment to renting. It is possible that the zoning by-law prohibits renting but despite this renting is legally allowed. Generally speaking, this occurs when the home has been rented continuously from a time before the by-law was enacted.

(b) The prudent purchaser will wish to be satisfied that the terms of the tenancy are accurately listed in the offer or agreement of purchase and sale.

(c) It will be necessary for the parties to make an adjustment for the amounts of money paid by the tenant. An example of this type of adjustment is shown on the statement of adjustments in Sample #12. This example considers the situation where there is only one tenant. In the situation where there are several tenants, a schedule of tenancies will usually be prepared and attached to the statement of adjustments.

17. Utilities

The vendor is responsible for paying and closing utility accounts, such as hydro, water, gas and telephone. It is up to the purchaser to arrange for the desired utilities to be connected under his or her name.

It is a common procedure for a purchaser to request and for a vendor to deliver an "undertaking" (promise on paper) on the closing of a residential real estate transaction whereby the vendor promises to pay all of the utility charges until the day of closing.

18. Transfer of insurance

Some residential real estate transactions involve the transfer or assignment of the fire insurance policy from the vendor to the purchaser at the time of closing. This requires the consent of the insurance company.

Since the transfer is usually delivered on the closing of the transaction and forwarded to the insurance company or the insurance agent to obtain consent, there will be a lapse of time between the closing and the time at which the insurance company endorses its consent on the insurance transfer. If the home should be destroyed by fire during this period, it may be that neither the purchaser nor the vendor are protected under the insurance policy.

In order to prevent this possibility, it is wise to advise the insurance company of the details prior to closing and to obtain their agreement to protect the interest of the purchaser after closing until they receive the insurance transfer or assignment. They will generally agree to this "hold covered" and to the transfer or assignment of the insurance policy.

19. Closing the transaction

As previously mentioned, the closing of a residential real estate transaction is largely governed by the provisions of the offer or agreement of purchase and sale and most, if not all, of the obligations of the parties are discharged on the completion of the transaction.

SAMPLE #12
STATEMENT OF ADJUSTMENTS

VENDOR SALE TO PURCHASER,
1234 ANY STREET, TORONTO

ADJUSTED AS OF JUNE 30, 1985[1]

SALE PRICE		$42 800.00
DEPOSIT	$ 2 000.00	
FIRST MORTGAGE ASSUMED		
Principal as of June 20, 1985[2]	24 851.17	
Interest to date of closing[3]	111.73	
SECOND MORTGAGE BACK	6 200.00	
1985 REALTY TAXES		
Total taxes	$1 016.26[4]	
Vendor's portion	503.95[5]	
Vendor has paid	796.26	
ALLOW VENDOR		292.31[6]

FIRE INSURANCE
Policy no. IOU626 of the
Faithful Insurance Company,
$33 000.00 coverage for 3
years expiring June 30, 1987
Premium of $150.00 paid.

ALLOW VENDOR		100.00

FUEL OIL
200 litres at 24.9¢ per litre[7]

ALLOW VENDOR		49.80

TENANCY
Tom Tenant in upstairs flat.
Monthly tenant (no written lease)
at $150.00 per month payable on
1st day of month. Rent paid to
June 30, 1985. No adjustment.[8]

PREPAID RENT
Tom Tenant in upstairs flat, one
month's prepaid rent.[9]

ALLOW PURCHASER	150.00	

BALANCE DUE ON CLOSING
(payable as follows)
1) To Marvin Mortgagee — $5 286.12[10]
2) To Lawyer and Lawyer —   30.00
3) To Conscientious Real Estate — 568.00[11]
4) To New House Builders Limited
        the balance[12] $ 9 929.21[13]
                                     _____
                                     $43 242.11 $43 242.11
                                                   ===========

E. & O.E.

NOTES TO SAMPLE #12:

[1]This is the date of adjustment. It is usually the same date as the date of closing and the date upon which possession is transferred, although these three matters may occur on three different dates. From the adjustment date onwards, the purchaser pays the costs of the home.

[2]The principal balance under the mortgage being assumed is as of the date of the last payment. This amount will usually be verified by a mortgage statement from the mortgagee.

[3]Mortgage interest, unlike rent, is not payable in advance but, rather, is payable at the end of the instalment period. If this mortgage is repayable in monthly instalments, the payment that is made on July 20, 1985 will include interest from June 20, 1985, and, since the vendor is responsible for the period from June 20, 1985 to June 30, 1985, the vendor must allow mortgage interest for this period to the purchaser.

[4]This is the total amount of realty taxes assessed against the property for the calendar year. Since this figure may not be known until as late as May or June, real estate transactions that are adjusted at an earlier date are usually adjusted on the basis of using the total taxes for the previous year as the estimated taxes for the current year and subsequently readjusting this item when the actual amount of taxes is known.

[5]This amount is obtained by multiplying the total taxes by the number of days for which the vendor is responsible and then dividing this product by the number of days in the year. This is

the dollar amount of realty taxes for which the vendor is responsible.

[6]This amount is calculated by subtracting the amount of the vendor's responsibility from the amount of taxes that the vendor has actually paid. Of course, when the vendor has paid less than the amount of his responsibility, the adjustment will be in favor of the purchaser.

[7]Since it is difficult if not impossible, to accurately determine the amount of fuel oil that remains in the tank as of closing, the practice has developed whereby the vendor will fill the fuel oil tank on the date of closing, pay this bill, and, then, receive credit for a full oil tank on the statement of adjustments.

[8]This is an adjustment of rent only and if the tenant is responsible for payment of other charges, these other charges would be included in the statement of adjustments and allowed accordingly. In this example, no adjustment of rent is made, however, since rent is usually payable in advance, if any adjustment is made, the amount will usually be allowed to the purchaser.

[9]This is not an adjustment of the current rent account but is an adjustment of *prepaid* rent only. Prepaid rent is sometimes called a "security deposit" but, in Ontario, a residential tenant is not required to pay a "security deposit" but may be required to pay the last month's rent in advance.

[10]These first two items indicate that the vendor is paying off a previous mortgage out of the funds received on closing and by directing the purchaser to pay these amounts directly to the mortgagee and his solicitors, delivery of a Discharge of Mortgage may be expedited. For a fuller discussion of how these amounts are calculated and the procedure in removing a mortgage encumbrance, see chapter 5.

[11]This amount represents payment of the balance of real estate commission payable to the real estate agent. In this example, the real estate commission is 6% of the sale price and the deposit paid by the purchaser is to be retained by the real estate agent, to be applied toward real estate commission.

[12]In this example, the vendor is also completing home purchase from New House Builders on the same day and rather than receiving the funds from the sale transaction, depositing this cheque and writing a new cheque, the more convenient way is to have the purchaser make his cheque payable to New House Builders directly.

[13]This is the exact amount to be paid by the purchaser and reflects all of the adjustments. If the funds are to be paid as set forth on the statement of adjustments, it will be necessary for the vendor to sign a direction, as set forth in Sample #14.

The purchaser's lawyer is concerned with three areas of the transaction on the closing, which are the title, possession and a proper accounting for the funds paid by the purchaser.

The purchaser's lawyer's job is to ensure that the purchaser is obtaining the title that is agreed to in the offer or agreement of purchase and sale, subject to any deficiencies that the purchaser may subsequently (but prior to closing) authorize and accept.

The purchaser's lawyer should make sure that all of the requisitions as to title have been answered; that there are no liens or encumbrances outstanding on the title and that the conveyance (the deed or transfer) is proper and sufficient in all respects prior to registration, of course.

In addition, if there are any deviations from the offer or agreement of purchase and sale, such as the agreement to pay funds to someone other than the vendor, the purchaser's lawyer will wish to obtain a written acknowledgment or direction confirming the deviation.

With regard to possession, the purchaser's lawyer will want to make sure that his or her client is obtaining possession in accordance with the offer or agreement of purchase and sale, which is usually the closing date. The transfer of a key from the vendor to the purchaser is the usual manner in which a change of possession is made and, accordingly, the purchaser's lawyer will insist upon either receiving a key on closing day or upon arrangements being made for the delivery of the key to the client that are satisfactory.

In new homes, the key is usually delivered by the vendor to the purchaser directly at the construction site on the day of closing. In older homes, a key is usually delivered from the vendor's lawyer to the purchaser's lawyer on closing day. If a tenancy is involved in the transaction, the purchaser's lawyer will usually ascertain the location of a duplicate key to the premises occupied by the tenant.

With regard to the accounting between the parties, the purchaser's lawyer should inspect the statement of adjustments prior to closing and check it for accuracy. The purchaser's lawyer should also obtain satisfactory evidence that the vendor has paid all items that the vendor has claimed to have paid and this evidence is usually in the form of receipts. For example, in the sample transaction set forth in the statement of adjustments in Sample #12, the purchaser's lawyer should obtain the following:

(a) A mortgage statement, signed by the first mortgagee, certifying that the principal balance owing under the first mortgage as of June 20, 1985 was $24 851.17.

(b) The tax bill or tax bills showing a total tax liability of $1 016.26 and a receipt for payment of $796.26 of this amount

(c) A receipt from the insurance agent indicating that the premium of $150 has been paid and a transfer or assignment of the insurance policy

(d) A receipt, or at least an invoice and an undertaking to pay the invoice, indicating that the fuel oil tank has been filled on the date of closing or on a date shortly before

If the purchaser's lawyer does not receive all of the above items, he or she will usually request and receive an undertaking on behalf of the vendor to pay the outstanding amount, if necessary, and to re-adjust the item on the statement of adjustments, if necessary.

20. Retail sales tax, land transfer tax and land speculation tax

The Retail Sales Tax Act (Ontario) imposes a tax on the purchaser of personal property (or chattels as they are sometimes referred to). To illustrate, a stove that is merely plugged into an electrical socket is probably taxable as a chattel but a stove that is built into the kitchen (in a more permanent way) is probably not taxable because it is a fixture and becomes part of the real estate itself.

In many residential real estate transactions, the purchaser will buy from the vendor certain items that he or she wants with the home. Common examples are a stove, refrigerator, washer, dryer, dishwasher, curtains, rugs and outdoor furniture. Usually the purchase price for these chattels (when they are chattels) is included in the price of the home.

Despite this, the Retail Sales Act requires that the total purchase price must be divided between the real estate and the chattel property, and the tax is imposed upon the portion of the purchase price that is paid for the chattel property.

If the value of the chattel property is greater than $100, this tax is payable at the time of the registration of the deed or transfer. A wise purchaser will include the allocation between chattels and real estate in the agreement of purchase and sale and will value the chattels at as low an amount as possible (since land transfer tax is less than retail sales tax for a Canadian resident); the vendor will not usually mind as long as the total purchase price is satisfactory.

The Land Transfer Tax Act imposes a tax on the purchaser of real property at the time of registration of the deed or transfer. This tax is paid to the Land Registrar who, in turn, forwards the amount to the government of Ontario. To guarantee that the tax is paid, the deed or transfer is not acceptable for registration unless it complies with the Land Transfer Tax Act.

This usually requires both the swearing of an affidavit and the payment of the tax. In most cases, the Land Transfer Tax Act will be complied with by an affidavit sworn by the purchaser or his or her lawyer showing the purchase price and how it is paid (that is, by cash, assumption of mortgage, mortgage back, land exchange, etc.). An example of this affidavit is contained in Sample #8.

You will note that the Land Transfer Tax Act affidavit requires that two allocations be made — the first being an allocation of the total purchase price as between the value of the real estate and the value of the chattel property and the second being an allocation of the amount paid for the real estate as between the various sources of payment.

Under the Land Transfer Tax Act a substantially greater amount is payable by people who are not residents of

Canada including corporations. A non-resident person includes "an individual who is not ordinarily resident in Canada and who, if ordinarily resident in Canada is neither a Canadian citizen nor an individual who has been lawfully admitted to Canada for permanent residence in Canada."

Thus, in order to be eligible for the payment of the lower rate of land transfer tax, two elements must be present as far as the purchaser is concerned:

(a) The purchaser must be either a Canadian citizen or a person who has been lawfully admitted to Canada for permanent residence in Canada.

(b) The purchaser must be "ordinarily resident in Canada" and the Land Transfer Tax Act considers the following to be people who are "ordinarily resident in Canada":

(i) A person lawfully admitted to Canada for permanent residence in Canada

(ii) A person who has sojourned in Canada for an aggregate of 366 days or more during the immediately preceding period of 24 months

(iii) A member of the Canadian Forces required to reside outside of Canada

(iv) An ambassador, minister, high commissioner, officer or servant of Canada or of a province of Canada who resided in Canada immediately prior to such employment or appointment

(v) A person working under an international development assistance program of the government of Canada (as so described in the Income Tax Act) who resided in Canada at any time in the three-month period preceding the day on which such services commenced

(vi) The spouse or child of a person described in the last three sub-paragraphs

There are three levels of taxation under the Land Transfer Tax Act. The first level is the "non-resident" rate of taxation, which is 20% of the purchase price of the property. As mentioned elsewhere, this non-resident level

159

of taxation is not applicable when the non-resident is buying land defined as "unrestricted" land. The second level of taxation is the basic level which consists of two steps — the first step is the rate of $5 per $1 000 of the purchase price, up to $55 000 and the second step is $10 per $1 000 of the purchase price above $55 000. The third level of taxation applies to resident taxpayers or to non-resident purchasers of unrestricted land and occurs if the property contains at least one and not more than two single family residences and the price is in excess of $250 000, in which event a surtax of an additional $10 for each $1 000 of the purchase price in excess of $250 000 is imposed.

By way of example, assume that a house is sold for $300 000 and that the allocation of that price is $295 000 for land and building and $5 000 for chattels. This property would likely qualify as "unrestricted land" but, for the purposes of our example, let us assume that it does not qualify. The non-resident purchaser would be required to pay the following upon registration of the transfer/deed of land:

(a) Retail sales tax (7% of $5 000) $ 350.00
(b) Land Transfer Tax:
    — basic amount (20% of $295 000.00)   59 000.00
    Total $ 59 350.00

The resident taxpayer would be required to pay the following upon registration of the transfer/deed of land:

(a) Retail sales tax (7% of $5 000) $ 350.00
(b) Land transfer tax:
    — basic amount, first step ($5 x 55)   275.00
    — basic amount, second step ($10 x 240)   2 400.00
    — surtax amount   450.00
    Total $ 3 475.00

A purchaser of real property is required to swear an affidavit of residency and of the value of the consideration. An example of this affidavit is shown as the last page of Sample #8, the transfer/deed of land. If this affidavit is not produced, the non-resident rate of tax is charged on the registration of the transfer/deed of land.

Although there are other provisions of the new Land Transfer Tax Act, only one of these need be mentioned as important to the residential real estate market. This provision is that the land transfer tax is payable upon the registration of a final order of foreclosure. Thus, if you sell a property in Ontario, take back a mortgage and later foreclose on the mortgage, land transfer tax is payable. If you lose your eligibility for the lower rate of tax between the time that the mortgage is obtained and the time that the mortgage is foreclosed, the payment of land transfer tax can be a substantial burden.

There is, however, a provision in the Land Transfer Tax Act whereby the Minister of Revenue may rebate to the person who registers the final order of foreclosure the tax paid by him or her, if —

(a) the land obtained by the foreclosure is sold within three years after the date of the final order of foreclosure, and

(b) the land is sold to a person who is a resident.

There is also provision for a partial rebate of the tax for such a sale of part of the land obtained by foreclosure.

21. Statement of trust account

A lawyer is obliged to supply to the client a statement of the monies that have been received and disbursed through his or her trust account. This statement will appear either in the reporting letter or as an additional statement following the lawyer's statement of account.

22. Lawyer's report

Following the completion of the transaction, the purchaser will receive a reporting letter from the lawyer. Each lawyer has his or her own style of reporting letter but most of them will usually cover the following areas:

(a) The lawyer's opinion as to state of the purchaser's title

(b) The matters pertaining to the accounting between the purchaser and the vendor

(c) Matters pertaining to the accounting· between the lawyer and the purchaser

A sample reporting letter to a real estate purchaser is shown in Sample #13. It must be remembered that this reporting letter is merely a sample and that other reporting letters may differ substantially.

e. SERVICES PROVIDED BY THE VENDOR'S LAWYER

1. Introduction

The nature and extent of the services provided by the purchaser's lawyer were discussed in the preceding section. Many of the services provided by the vendor's lawyer were also discussed. To fully appreciate the roles of both lawyers, these two sections should be read together.

The purchaser's lawyer is primarily concerned with title; the vendor's lawyer is primarily concerned with a proper accounting between the parties. In order to do this he or she must be supplied with certain documents. You can save yourself time by collecting together the following information and delivering it to your lawyer when delivering the signed offer.

(a) The deed

(b) The survey

(c) Any other title documents that the vendor has, such as a declaration of possession

(d) A copy of the mortgage and a copy of the vendor's accounting of the mortgage

(e) Insurance policy or policies

(f) Realty tax bills for the current year and the past years

(g) Water and sewage account

(h) If the transaction is such that the vendor is assigning a tenancy or tenancies to the purchaser, a list and details of the tenancies

(i) The method of heating the premises and, if the premises are heated by oil, the capacity of the fuel oil tank

SAMPLE #13
LAWYER'S REPORT TO PURCHASER

BARRISTER AND SOLICITOR
Barristers and Solicitors,
100 LEGAL LANE,
Toronto, Ontario

July 7, 198-

Mr. and Ms. P. Purchaser,
1234 Any Street,
Toronto, Ontario

Dear Mr. and Ms. Purchaser:

RE: PURCHASER PURCHASE FROM VENDOR,
1234 ANY STREET, TORONTO

As you know, the above transaction has been completed and we are pleased to report to you as follows:

TITLE
Pursuant to the Agreement of Purchase and Sale, you purchased the property municipally known as 1234 Any Street, Toronto, being the whole of Lot number 62, Plan 10572, City of Toronto. Upon the closing of this transaction, a Deed was registered in favor of:

PETER PURCHASER, of the City of Toronto, in the Municipality of Metropolitan Toronto, Esquire, and PAULA PURCHASER, his wife, of the same place, as joint tenants and not as tenants in common.

In our professional opinion, you have a good and marketable title to these lands and premises, subject only to what is hereinafter set forth.

SURVEY
The survey of the above property was prepared by Messrs. Read and Write, Ontario Land Surveyors, and was dated May 29, 1952. We discussed this survey with you and you instructed us that you did not wish to have a new survey of the property prepared and, accordingly, the above transaction was completed on this basis.

DECLARATION OF POSSESSION

On the closing of the above transaction, we received a Declaration of Possession of Victor Vendor for the period from June 5, 1985 to the date of closing and we enclose same herewith.

FIRST MORTGAGE

Upon the closing of the above transaction, you assumed a first mortgage in favor of The Life Insurance Company which mortgage was in the principal amount of $24 851.71 as of June 20, 1985, bears interest at the rate of 9½% per annum, calculated half-yearly, not in advance and is repayable in equal blended monthly instalments of $362.48, which includes both principal and interest, and these instalments are due on the 20th day of each and every month in each and every year, from and including July 20, 1985, to and including October 20, 1990 when the mortgage matures.

Payments under this mortgage are to be sent to 789 Payout Court.

You will note on the Statement of Adjustments that you were given credit for the full amount of the outstanding principal under this mortgage. You were also given credit for the interest on this mortgage from June 20, 1985 to the date of closing, June 30, 1985.

We are enclosing herein a loan amortization schedule in order to assist you in keeping track of the payments under this mortgage. We also enclose a copy of this mortgage for your records.

SECOND MORTGAGE

In accordance with the Agreement of Purchase and Sale, you gave Violet Vendor a second mortgage in the principal sum of $6 200.00. This mortgage bears interest at the rate of 8½% per annum and is repayable in quarterly instalments of $100.00 on account of principal plus interest and these instalments are to be paid on the 30th days of September and December, 1985 and on the 30th days of March, June, September and December in the years 1986, 1987, 1988, 1989 and 1990, and on the 30th day of March, 1990 and this mortgage matures on the 30th day of June, 1990.

This mortgage contains the following privileges, as more particularly described in the mortgage document:

1) You may prepay the whole or any part of the principal sum at any time or times without notice or bonus;

2) You may renew the second mortgage for a further period of 4 years only, provided that the interest rate during the renewal period will be 10½%;

3) You may renew or replace the first mortgage, at its maturity, provided that any additional principal obtained by you at that time will be payable to the second mortgagee in reduction of the second mortgage account and provided that the interest rate on such renewal or replacement first mortgage shall not exceed 10%.

Payments under this mortgage are to be made in favor of Violet Vendor and sent to her at 1236 Any Street, Toronto, Ontario.

We enclose herewith a loan payment schedule with respect to this mortgage and we also enclose an office copy of this mortgage, for your records.

REALTY TAXES

The 1985 realty taxes for the above property were $1 016.26. The vendor was responsible for $503.95 of these taxes and, since the vendor had paid $796.26, the vendor was allowed $292.31 on the Statement of Adjustments.

FIRE INSURANCE

Pursuant to the Agreement of Purchase and Sale, you received on closing the fire insurance policy described in the Statement of Adjustments. You will note that the vendor had paid the entire premium for this policy but was only responsible for the first year of this premium. Accordingly, the vendor has allowed the sum of $100.00 on the Statement of Adjustments.

A certified copy of this policy will be forwarded to you in due course. Upon receipt of same, we would suggest that you contact your insurance agent in order to fully discuss your insurance requirements.

FUEL OIL
On the closing of the above transaction, you purchased from the vendor 200 litres of fuel oil and, accordingly, the vendor was allowed the sum of $49.80 in this regard.

TENANCY
Pursuant to the Agreement of Purchase and Sale, you purchased the above property subject to the tenancy of the upstairs flat by Tom Tenant, who is a monthly tenant with no written lease. This tenant pays $150.00 per month and these rental payments are payable in advance on the first day of each and every month. We have been advised that the rent has been paid up to and including June 30, 1985, and, accordingly, no adjustment was made on the Statement of Adjustments with regard to current rent. However, the tenant had prepaid the last month's rent under the tenancy and, accordingly, you were allowed the sum of $150.00 on the Statement of Adjustments in this regard.

CHANGE OF OWNERSHIP
We have advised the City of Toronto Assessment Office of your purchase of the above property and have asked that they amend their records accordingly.

STATEMENT OF TRUST ACCOUNT
Prior to the closing of the above transaction, you provided us with a certified cheque in the amount of $10 683.61. Out of these funds, we paid the following:

1) The sum of $9 929.21 to the Direction of the Vendor, as shown on the Statement of Adjustments;

2) We retained the remaining $754.40 in payment of our Statement of Account, which is enclosed herewith.

ENCLOSURES
We enclose herewith the following:

1) Deed, in your favor;

2) Copy of first mortgage;

3) Copy of second mortgage;

4) Copy of survey;

5) Copy of Declaration of Possession;

6) Copy of Mortgage Statement;

7) Our Statement of Account.

If you have any questions with respect to the above, please do not hesitate to contact us.

Yours very truly

BARRISTER AND SOLICITOR

JOHN A. BARRISTER

JAB/HR
encls.

When your lawyer has received the preceding information, he or she can begin to prepare the transaction for the closing. One of the first things he or she will usually do is provide the purchaser's lawyer with the registration particulars of the property so that a search of the title may be carried out. In addition, a copy of the survey, if any, will be sent to the purchaser's lawyer. Following this, a statement of adjustments will be prepared and a copy sent to the purchaser's lawyer.

2. Title

The lawyer for the vendor is concerned with the matter of title to the premises for two reasons:

(a) To satisfy the purchaser that the vendor has the title claimed in the agreement of purchase and sale

(b) To satisfy the purchaser that the conveyance from the vendor to the purchaser is a good and proper conveyance

To do this, the vendor's lawyer will first answer the requisitions submitted by the purchaser's lawyer; then he or she will prepare a deed from the vendor to the purchaser and will send a copy to the purchaser's lawyer.

If the purchaser's lawyer is not happy with the answer to the requisition, he or she may apply to have the court determine whether it has been satisfactorily answered. This type of proceeding is beyond the scope of this book.

3. Accounting between the parties

The statement of adjustments has been discussed previously, and a sample of a statement of adjustments is shown in Sample #12.

The vendor's lawyer prepares the statement of adjustments. If the lawyer can get the receipts for all the items described in the statement from the vendor, then the transaction can be closed with no further undertakings. Undertakings are discussed later in this section.

You will note from the sample statement of adjustments that the largest item of adjustment is the first mortgage and this is common in residential real estate transactions. Of course, a receipt for previous mortgage payments is usually not available. However, a mortgage statement serves the same purpose.

The mortgage statement is necessary when the purchaser is assuming the mortgage (see Sample #11).

When the statement of adjustments has been prepared, two copies will be sent to the purchaser's lawyer. It is a good idea to do this well before closing so that the purchaser will know the exact amount of money required on closing and will be able to arrange his or her affairs.

4. Utilities

Utilities, such as water, hydro, gas and telephone, should be cancelled by the vendor as of the date of closing of the transaction. If the utility accounts are not cancelled, the vendor may be responsible for the payment of charges incurred after the date of closing. The vendor usually takes care of this.

If the premises are heated by oil, the most common way of accounting for the supply of fuel oil is for the vendor to have the fuel oil tank filled as of the date of closing and to pay the cost of filling the tank at this time. The purchaser is charged for this in the statement of adjustments.

5. Insurance

As previously mentioned, insurance is considered by many lawyers to be one of the most important items pertaining to a real estate transaction. In all transactions, the lawyer for the purchaser is the one who is concerned about the existence of insurance and that the coverage is adequate. If the purchaser is giving back a mortgage to the vendor, both the lawyer for the purchaser and the lawyer for the vendor will be concerned about the insurance protection. If a mortgagee is involved, the mortgagee will also be concerned about the insurance coverage.

In the current practice, the most common type of insurance policy for a dwelling, the home owners policy, is not transferable and, therefore, in most transactions the vendor will merely cancel his or her insurance coverage or will have the coverage amended to cover the vendor's new home or apartment, leaving the purchaser to arrange to obtain the requisite policy. In these circumstances, since the insurance arrangements are being made at or near the time of closing, it has become quite common that an insurance policy is not able to be produced on closing but, rather, the parties are forced to rely on a certificate or binder letter from the insurance agent or broker that the coverage has, in fact, been placed and arranged until the actual policy is provided by the insurance company, which can be a month or more after the closing.

If the vendor will be vacating the premises before the closing of the transaction, he or she should obtain a vacancy permit which is endorsed on the policy and ensures that insurance coverage does not lapse while the premises are vacant (i.e., vacant premises represent a higher risk for insurers than occupied premises).

If the vendor is taking a mortgage back, his or her lawyer will wish to make sure that the amount of insurance coverage against fire and other extended perils is large enough to cover the total amount of mortgage including the mortgage back in favor of the vendor. For example, if the vendor is selling the home for $40 000, of which $20 000 is represented by a first mortgage being assumed by the purchaser and $5 000 is represented by a mortgage back in favor of the vendor, the vendor's lawyer will wish to make sure that there is $25 000 of fire insurance on the property as of the date of closing. Land is not to be insured, however, and therefore the maximum amount of insurance that is likely to be available is the cost of replacing the house.

6. Discharging existing mortgages

If the agreement of purchase and sale does not provide for the assumption of all existing mortgages by the purchaser and if the vendor requires some of the proceeds of the sale in order to pay the balance of the existing mortgagee's account, it will be necessary for the purchaser's lawyer to make arrangements with the mortgagee and with the vendor's lawyer to obtain and register this discharge of mortgage. This situation has been previously discussed.

The most common procedure is for the vendor's lawyer to obtain from the mortgagee a mortgage statement for discharge purposes. When this statement has been obtained, he or she will direct the purchaser to make the necessary funds payable to the mortgagee. This is done in a "direction regarding funds" which is shown in Sample #14.

Thus, on the closing of the transaction illustrated by Sample #14, the purchaser would pay the funds through both lawyers to Marvin Mortgagee and the discharge of mortgage would be registered subsequent to the closing.

7. Residency in Canada

See chapter 5 for a discussion of section 116 of the Income Tax Act. Briefly, if the vendor has been a resident of Canada until the time of the closing, there is usually no problem with regard to this particular requirement, other than providing satisfactory evidence to the purchaser's lawyer. The standard forms of agreement of purchase and sale now

DIRECTION REGARDING FUNDS

TO: PETER PURCHASER AND PAULA PURCHASER

AND TO: BARRISTER AND SOLICITOR, THEIR SOLICITORS

RE: VENDOR SALE TO PURCHASER
1234 ANY STREET, TORONTO

DIRECTION

You are hereby authorized and directed to pay the balance due on closing in the above transaction, as follows:

1) To Marvin Mortgagee	$5 286.12
2) To Lawyer and Lawyer	30.00
3) To Conscientious Real Estate	568.00
4) To New House Builders Limited	— the balance,

and, for so doing, this shall be your good and sufficient authority.

DATED at Toronto, this 28th day of June, 1985.

(signed) _Victor Vendor._

cover in detail the procedure for satisfying the requirements of section 116 of the Income Tax Act and, in the most common case (where the vendor is a Canadian resident), a sworn statement to this effect will suffice.

However, if the vendor is going to be a non-resident at closing, as a part of the preparation for closing, the vendor's lawyer should prepare the application for the appropriate certificate and submit it to Revenue Canada and obtain the certificate prior to closing. The process takes several weeks and should be addressed early in the preparation. The certificate, when issued, will establish a limit in the price that the purchaser may pay to the vendor without being exposed to a liability for the payment of additional tax. This does not mean that there is a limit that the purchaser can pay for the property but this is a limit which, if not exceeded, will ensure that the purchaser has no further liability for this type of tax.

8. Deviations from the agreement of purchase and sale

Any deviation from the terms of the agreement of purchase and sale that is agreeable to both parties may be done through "directions" from one party to the other party, rather than through an agreement amending the agreement of purchase and sale.

A common example is a direction regarding funds. In the standard form agreement of purchase and sale, the purchaser is required to pay the additional amount on closing to the vendor and, if the vendor wishes to have the balance due on closing paid in any other manner, the purchaser, if he or she is willing, will insist upon and require a direction authorizing this deviation from the agreement of purchase and sale.

A direction regarding funds is the most common direction produced in a residential real estate transaction. Many of these directions require the purchaser to pay the funds to the solicitor for the vendor. In this way, the solicitor for the vendor can satisfy all of the vendor's financial obligations resulting from the closing of the transaction and forward the balance remaining to the vendor.

For example, on the closing of a residential real estate transaction, it is not uncommon for the vendor to be liable for a premium for increased insurance coverage, outstanding mortgage accounts, real estate commission and lawyer's fees and disbursements.

Another common direction regarding the payment of funds arises in the situation when a vendor is also purchasing a new home on the same day as selling the old home. This type of direction regarding the payment of funds will direct the purchaser of the old home to pay the funds in favor of the vendor of the new home and, thus, will avoid the necessity of depositing the funds from the sale of the old home into a bank account and subsequently drawing a cheque for the amount of money required to purchase the new home.

This latter situation is illustrated in Samples #12 and #14, where the vendors have directed that a portion of the balance due on closing should be paid to New House Builders.

Another common situation is where a vendor has arranged to sell a mortgage back at the time of closing of the sale transaction. Since this is a deviation from the agreement of purchase and sale, a direction authorizing the purchasers to draft the mortgage in this manner must be produced by the vendor on the closing of the transaction.

In the example in Sample #15, the vendors have agreed to sell the second mortgage back to a third party and all parties have agreed to having the mortgage prepared directly from the purchasers to this third party.

9. The closing

On the closing of a residential real estate transaction, the vendor's lawyer will wish to obtain the following:

- (a) A certified cheque or cheques in the total amount of the balance due on closing, payable in accordance with the vendor's direction
- (b) Any directions required to authorize deviations from the terms of the agreement of purchase and sale
- (c) The mortgage back, if any

The vendor's lawyer will usually have to give to the purchaser's lawyer the following:

- (a) An executed deed
- (b) Any documents arising out of the requisitions made by the purchaser's lawyer
- (c) Any directions that are necessary due to deviations from the agreement of purchase and sale
- (d) Bills, receipts, acknowledgments from tenants and a mortgage statement, if required, in support of the items contained on the statement of adjustments.

173

(e) The fire insurance policies indicated on the statement of adjustments and a transfer of the fire insurance policies

(f) Possession (It is most common for the vendor's lawyer to provide a key on the closing of the transaction to the purchaser's lawyer.)

In order to be able to register the deed or transfer, certain affidavits must be sworn. One of these affidavits is an affidavit of compliance with the Planning Act.

Your lawyer should discuss the matter of writs of execution prior to closing. If the vendor indicates that there are no writs of execution against him or her, the vendor's lawyer will usually prepare an affidavit to this effect for the vendor to sign.

If the purchaser's lawyer discovers that there is an outstanding execution against a person with a name similar to the vendor, the statutory declaration will be available to show that the vendor is not the same person as the execution creditor. In some situations, this statutory declaration will be satisfactory. In other cases, evidence will be required to be provided from the judgment creditor or his or her lawyer. Often, this requirement is discovered too close to closing in order to allow sufficient time to obtain the requisite evidence. In these cases, it is often necessary to delay the closing or to close in escrow in order to permit this evidence to be obtained.

If problems arise on the closing of the residential real estate transaction and if the requirements of the parties are such that they require the funds or possession on the date of closing, the transaction may be completed in escrow.

A closing in escrow is, in effect, a closing of a transaction, subject to the remaining outstanding matters in the transaction being completed. In this situation, it is common that an escrow agreement is executed by the parties or their lawyers, putting their closing arrangements in writing.

DIRECTION REGARDING SECOND MORTGAGE

TO: PETER PURCHASER AND PAULA PURCHASER

AND TO: BARRISTER AND SOLICITOR, THEIR SOLICITORS

RE: VENDOR SALE TO PURCHASER
1234 ANY STREET, TORONTO

DIRECTION

You are hereby authorized and directed to describe the Mortgagee in the second Mortgage being given back on the closing of the above transaction as follows:

"VIOLET VENDOR, of the City of Toronto, in the Municipality of Metropolitan Toronto, Married Woman"

and, for so doing, this shall be your good and sufficient authority.

DATED at Toronto, this 28th day of June, 1985.

(signed) _Victor Vendor._

An example where an escrow closing may occur is as follows:

An execution against Viola V. Vendor has been filed on the day before the closing of the sale transaction of 123 Any Street by Victor and Verna Vendor to Peter and Paula Purchaser and, in order to register the transfer/deed of land in the land registry office, an affidavit must be sworn by Verna Vendor and filed with the transfer/deed of land. Victor and Verna are in the process of moving from their old house to the new house that they have purchased and are unable to see their lawyer until very late in the day. In addition, Peter and Paula Purchaser have completed filling their moving van and are in the process of moving into 123

Any Street. All other matters relating to the transaction are satisfactory.

In this situation, if all of the parties are agreeable, the transaction may be closed in escrow on the agreement by the parties, through their lawyers, that Verna will make arrangements to see her lawyer during the evening of the day of closing to swear the necessary affidavit. The affidavit will then be delivered to the lawyer for Peter and Paula Purchaser on the next day for filing with the transfer/deed of land. This agreement will provide that if the transfer/deed of land is not registered, as anticipated, Peter and Paula Purchaser will be entitled to a return of the monies paid by them and Peter and Paula Purchaser will give up possession of the home.

10. Undertakings (promises to do things after closing)

An undertaking given on the closing of a residential real estate transaction is an obligation that a party agrees to fulfill after the closing of the transaction.

For example, the total charges for utility services are not usually known until after the transaction has been completed because a final reading of the utility meter must be made on the date of closing. The purchaser, of course, will not wish to pay any utility charges for the period prior to closing and will usually request an undertaking from the vendor that the vendor will pay all utility charges incurred up to the date of closing.

Another example of an undertaking given on closing occurs when the vendor has not supplied all of the receipts for the items contained on the statement of adjustments. Then, it is common for the transaction to be completed on the basis of the vendor providing an undertaking to readjust that item of the statement of adjustments, if necessary.

11. Notifying the tax authorities

In order to amend the tax records to reflect the sale of real estate, it is necessary for a letter to be written and sent to the tax department for the municipality in which the land is located and to the relevant provincial assessment office.

176

This is usually done by the vendor's lawyer following the closing of the transaction.

12. Loan payment schedule (for mortgage accounting)

If the vendor is receiving a mortgage back on closing, his or her lawyer will often obtain a "loan payment schedule."

This loan payment schedule is a computer calculation for the term of the mortgage which divides each payment into the amount of principal and the amount of interest and shows the balance of the principal outstanding after each payment is made. It is useful for keeping track of the mortgage account as each payment is made, for determining the amount of interest received for income tax purposes and for supplying a mortgage statement, as may be required. This schedule is relatively inexpensive and will usually be obtained as a matter of course.

13. Lawyer's report

The vendor's lawyer will provide a reporting letter following the closing of the transaction. The letter will usually detail the aspects of the transaction that are important to the vendor. These are, of course, the proceeds of the sale of the property and the accounting for the proceeds. An example of a reporting letter to a vendor is shown in Sample #16. The form and content of reporting letters differ from lawyer to lawyer.

SAMPLE #16
LAWYER'S REPORT TO VENDOR

ME AND YOU
Barristers and Solicitors
5678 Our Steet
Toronto, Ontario

July 7, 198-

Mr. V. Vendor
629571 Some Street
Scarborough, Ontario

Dear Mr. Vendor:

RE: VENDOR SALE TO PURCHASER
1234 ANY STREET, TORONTO

As you know, we have completed the above transaction on your behalf and are pleased to report to you as follows:

FUNDS:

Upon the closing of the above transaction and, in accordance with your instructions and Direction, certified cheques in the total amount of $9 929.21 were received on closing. These cheques were disbursed as follows:

1) To Marvin Mortgagee, with respect to obtaining a discharge of the second mortgage	$5 286.12
2) To Lawyer and Lawyer with respect to their discharge fee on the discharge of the second mortgage	30.00
3) To Conscientious Real Estate, in payment of the balance of real estate commission	568.00
4) To New House Builders Limited, with respect to the purchase of your new home	$4 045.09
TOTAL	$9 929.21

DEPOSIT

The deposit in the above transaction was paid to the real estate agent to be applied toward real estate commission payable upon the completion of the above transaction. You total liability for real estate commission was $2 568.00 and, pursuant to your instructions, we forwarded the remaining $568.00 to the real estate agent.

FIRST MORTGAGE

Upon the closing of the above transaction, the purchasers assumed your pre-existing first mortgage on the above property. The principal amount owing under the above first mortgage as of June 20, 1985 was $24 851.17 and interest thereon from June 20, 1985 to the date of closing, June 30, 1985 was in the amount of $111.73. The purchasers were allowed these amounts on the Statements of Adjustments.

SECOND MORTGAGE

Upon the closing of the above transaction, a second mortgage for $6 200.00 was to be given back to you, however, you agreed to sell this mortgage to your mother for the sum of $6 200.00 and, accordingly, this mortgage was made in favor of Violet Vendor, of the City of Toronto, in the Municipality of Metropolitan Toronto, Married Woman. We received the sum of $6 200.00 from your mother and the disbursement of this amount is shown on the Statement of Trust Account included in our Statement of Account. You will note that the purchasers were given credit on the Statement of Adjustments for the face amount of this second Mortgage.

1985 REALTY TAXES

The total 1985 realty taxes were in the amount of $1 016.26 and you had paid $796.26 of this amount. You were only responsible for $503.95 toward 1985 realty taxes and, accordingly, you were allowed the sum of $292.31 on the Statement of Adjustments in this regard.

FIRE INSURANCE

Upon the closing of the above transaction, you sold the fire insurance policy shown on the Statement of Adjustments to the purchasers. You had paid the entire premium of $150.00 for the three years of coverage under this policy and, accordingly, you were allowed the amount of $100.00 on the Statement of Adjustments as prepaid fire insurance premiums.

FUEL OIL

We advised you that you should fill the fuel oil tank on the date of closing and you informed us that you would attend to this matter. Accordingly, you were allowed the sum of $49.80 on the Statement of Adjustments with respect to the fuel oil, being a full tank containing 200 litres of fuel oil.

TENANCY

The purchasers assumed the tenancy in the upstairs flat of the above premises. Since the date of closing occurred on the same day as the last day of a rental period, no adjustment was necessary with respect to rent. However, you informed us that you had received from the tenant the amount of $150.00 as prepaid rent for the last month of the tenancy of this tenant and, accordingly, the purchasers were allowed this amount on the Statement of Adjustments.

STATEMENT OF ADJUSTMENTS

We enclose herewith a copy of the Statement of Adjustments in this transaction.

STATEMENT OF ACCOUNT AND
STATEMENT OF TRUST ACCOUNT

Our Statement of Account and Statement of Trust Account is enclosed herewith.

Yours very truly,

ME AND YOU

I. C. YOU

ICY: SR
encl.

9

YOUR HOME AND TAXES

a. CAPITAL GAINS TAX

One of the great benefits of home ownership is that the primary residence of a home owner is not subject to capital gains tax. Thus, if Harry and Hilda Homeseeker bought their home for $41 000, turn around two years later and sell their home for $62 000, the $21 000 increase would be tax free.

However, only the house and up to one acre surrounding the house are automatically tax free. When the house is situated on more than one acre, the general test applied by the tax department is, "Can the property over one acre reasonably be regarded as necessary for the use and enjoyment of the residence?" Such factors as the landscaping plan, location of the home on the property, and subdivision regulations of the local municipality are all considered.

It is no longer possible for a married couple to have two primary residences. In the past, if the couple owned a home as well as a piece of recreational property, for example, that was used often, it was possible to designate one as the primary residence of one spouse and the other as the primary residence of the other spouse for income tax purposes.

This possibility was eliminated in 1981. Now, only one family property qualifies for the capital gains exemption. (This applied to married couples only; so far, couples who live together are not affected.) So, any capital gains on a recreational property owned in addition to the family residence are taxable.

On the other hand, recreational property can be depreciated and expenses written off if you declare the property "commercial" by placing it on the rental market.

Most people do not use such property frequently and the tax write-offs gained may be well worth the inconvenience of having it available for rental purposes.

Talk it over with your accountant and get some figures on paper. Of course, if this is done, you lose the capital gain tax-free status but, despite this, the tax savings gained by converting the premises to commercial use can be substantial. This is especially so if you are paying interest on a mortgage (the major cost of any dwelling) which can then be written off.

As mentioned previously under the section dealing with vendor financing, some vendors are prepared to leave some of the equity in their primary residence when they sell it, provided the equity is secured by a mortgage. Any interest earned from such a mortgage is income. If a vendor finds that it is easier to sell a home by asking perhaps slightly more for the home but offering a lower interest rate or perhaps a longer term on the financing, that vendor would be much better off from a tax point of view even though the total amount paid by the purchaser would be the same. Of course, in considering this, the parties must keep in mind the inflation rate (the deteriorating value of the dollar). This would be so since the higher purchase price would be tax free, while the lower interest earned would mean less income tax to pay.

Likewise, in situations where the vendors of the house were joint owners but were in different income tax brackets, the sale should be structured in such a way that the person with the higher income tax bracket is fully paid out while the person with the lower income tax bracket provides the financing so that all interest income is taxed at the lower rate.

b. ARE YOU OPERATING A RENOVATIONS BUSINESS?

Jack Carpenter had discovered that he could buy an older run-down house, fix it up while living in it with his family, and then sell it and move on to the next old home that needed repairs. He had done so approximately six times in the last two years.

Suddenly, one day he received a reassessment from the tax department. They had taken all of the profits that he had made on all the houses that he had renovated since starting this method of operation and added it all back into his income, disagreeing with his allocation of profits as "capital gains." They then taxed him on these new figures.

By the frequency of his transactions, Jack had established that his intent was not just to live there but also to make money by fixing up the homes and selling them. The tax department had taken the position that what he was doing was a business and had taxed him accordingly.

What is the difference between this and the case where you fix your house and later find it is not to your liking? A sale here is not in the course of business and would be tax free. Probably the main factor is the number of times you buy and sell over a certain period. Once is okay, probably twice — but beyond that it gets tricky.

c. WHAT IF YOU RENT OUT YOUR HOME?

If you and your family are planning to travel or perhaps be away on an extended business trip you may be considering the possibility of renting your home. You must be careful about the tax implications in this case because the Income Tax Act says that, as soon as you rent your home, you are deemed to have disposed of it and, when you return, to have reacquired it at fair market value.

With the rapid rise in property value during these inflationary times, this will subject you to both a taxable capital gain as commercial property and a recapture of the capital cost allowance which you would be charging as an expense to offset the rental income.

Faced with this, you are probably better off making an election under section 45(2) of the Income Tax Act, which allows you to maintain your home as "principal residence" and thus keep it free of capital gains tax for up to four years even though you may not ordinarily "inhabit" the house. During this time you may not claim capital cost allowance and the rental income must be subject to tax. You are still allowed to charge against income the normal operating expenses such as heat, light, insurance, maintenance, mortgage interest, and taxes.

As long as you have not claimed any capital cost allowance you would normally be allowed to make this election after the rental period has started.

d. ARE YOU RENTING OUT PART OF YOUR HOME OR OPERATING A BUSINESS OUT OF IT?

You may be interested in renting out part of your home or, perhaps, operating a business out of the basement. In this case you must again be careful about the "principal" residence status of your home. Where part of the principal residence is set aside for the purpose of earning income, then a reasonable proportion of the expenses, such as utilities, insurance, mortgage interest, and taxes, can be deducted as expenses against your income.

You should be careful again, however, not to charge capital cost allowance, as this will change your property from residential to commercial and the house will lose its capital gains tax free status.

For more information, obtain the Interpretation Bulletin IT-20 from your nearest district taxation office.

e. MAKING YOUR MORTGAGE INTEREST TAX DEDUCTIBLE

Under normal circumstances, interest paid on a mortgage on the home is not a deductible expense for income tax purposes. However, interest expense incurred for the purpose of earning income is deductible. So, if a mortgage is taken out on the home, and all or part of the proceeds are used for investing, the interest on the mortgage applicable to such portion used for investing is deductible even if no income was in fact earned.

If a person, therefore, were to receive a large sum of money, it would be advantageous, rather than investing it directly, to pay off the mortgage, then refinance and invest. The interest on the mortgage would then be deductible.

10

MISCELLANEOUS MATTERS

a. EXPROPRIATION

It would be terrible to complete a real estate transaction and soon thereafter find that a portion or all of the property is to be expropriated. When buying a home, especially an older home in a metropolitan area where there is a likelihood of redevelopment, be sure to ask the vendor if there have been any expropriation discussions or negotiations. Include the vendor's answer on the offers as a warranty and representation of the vendor.

The problems relating to an actual expropriation of land are beyond the scope of this book. If you are involved in an expropriation, you will need professional advice.

b. WHAT HAPPENS IF YOUR MORTGAGE ISN'T PAID?

This section briefly considers the rights and obligations of the various parties when the mortgagor (borrower) is unwilling or unable to pay the mortgage instalments on time. This area of the law is extremely technical and complicated and, if this situation should occur, each party should seek the assistance of their legal advisor at the earliest possible date.

When a mortgagor defaults on the mortgage, the mortgagee (lender) has a right of action against the mortgagor personally or against the property.

If the mortgagee believes the mortgagor has sufficient assets that are readily available for seizure, he or she may decide to proceed against the mortgagor in a personal capacity only. In this case, the mortgagee does not look to the security of the property. However, this situation does not often occur and the mortgagee will usually look to the security of the land and buildings.

There are three types of proceedings available to a mortgagee to enforce the security even under the mortgage and he or she must choose the most appropriate course of action under the circumstances. They are as follows:

(a) Foreclosure
(b) Power of private sale
(c) Sale of the property by the court

1. Foreclosure

An action of foreclosure is a proceeding whereby the person who institutes the proceedings (the mortgagee), seeks to bar the rights of all *subsequent* encumbrancers of the property, including the mortgagor.

For example, David Debtor is a home owner who has given three mortgages on the property. In addition, after giving the mortgages, he has been sued by two of his creditors and also a construction lien has been registered against the property.

Suppose David Debtor then defaults on all three mortgages. In this case any of the mortgagees may start a foreclosure. Practically, the mortgagee lowest on the totem pole (in this case the third mortgagee) is pressured to begin the foreclosure. This is because the lowest mortgagee is the most likely to lose his or her security by virtue of a foreclosure or sale proceeding by the first or second mortgagee.

If the second mortgagee wishes to proceed in an action for foreclosure, the second mortgagee will be proceeding against the third mortgagee, the two execution creditors, the construction lien claimant and the home owner.

If the foreclosure proceedings are successful, the second mortgagee will obtain title to the property subject only to the rights of the first mortgagee. The rights of the third mortgagee, the two execution creditors, the construction lien claimant and the home owner will be extinguished.

This is a very simple example and does not consider all of the rights of redemption of the parties being barred but, rather, assumes that none of these parties wishes to take advantage of his or her rights in the property.

The successful party in a foreclosure action does not become entitled to possession of the property, but, rather, merely becomes the person entitled to the *legal title*. Thus, in addition to the order of foreclosure, the successful party must also obtain possession of the property. Possession may be obtained by an order of the court, and the sheriff will attend to the actual eviction. The successful party then has both title and possession and can proceed to sell the property to a new purchaser.

For more information, see *Mortgages and Foreclosure*, another title in the Self-Counsel Series.

2. Power of private sale

Alternatively, a mortgagee may decide to proceed by selling the property under the power of private sale contained in the mortgage if the mortgage, in fact, contains such a power. A "power of private sale" is, briefly, an agreement by the mortgagor in the mortgage whereby the mortgagee may sell or lease the property if the mortgagor is in default of paying the principal and interest under the mortgage.

No matter what is contained in the mortgage regarding the power of private sale, the Mortgages Act provides minimum requirements relating to a sale under a power of private sale contained in a mortgage. The standard form of mortgage in common use today, as supplied by the various stationers, contains a power of private sale which is usually consistent in all respects with the minimum requirements established by the Mortgages Act.

Before deciding to proceed this way, the mortgagee must first be satisfied that this is the best method of enforcing his or her rights. The main consideration here is whether or not the property will be able to be sold readily on the current real estate market for an amount sufficient to cover all prior encumbrances, all costs incidental to the sale of the property and a substantial portion of the mortgagee's claim.

The advantage under power of private sale is that if a satisfactory purchaser can be easily found, it will be the quickest method for the mortgagee to enforce his or her rights. It follows that if the sale under the power of sale can be completed within a short lapse of time, the mortgagor and the subsequent encumbrancers will have a shorter time in which they may bring the mortgage back into good standing.

As under a foreclosure action, a mortgagee selling under power of private sale must obtain possession of the property through the courts before possession can legally be conveyed to a third party.

In both these procedures, the mortgagor and the subsequent encumbrancers have a right to redeem (a right to satisfy the default of the defaulting party). The right to redeem exists until completion of the proceedings and, in some cases, afterwards.

3. Judicial sale

A third alternative available to a mortgagee is to proceed by way of a judicial sale of the security under the mortgage. In this manner of proceeding, the mortgagee submits the claim and the remedy for this claim to the supervision and authority of the court.

The court will then take control of the matter and will direct that various procedures be taken, such as the retaining of a real estate agent, and the sale will then be supervised and confirmed by way of court order.

A judicial sale does not relieve the mortgagee of the necessity of attempting to find a purchaser for the property, and the mortgagee must assist the court in this regard. However, under this method, the mortgagee is transferring the responsibility for the sale (and, therefore, any potential liability) to the court. In addition, under this procedure, it will not be necessary for the mortgagee to institute separate proceedings to obtain possession of the property.

Once the path has been picked, the mortgagor will receive, probably by way of personal service, a legal document indicating the mortgagee's intentions. At this time, the mortgagor is then in the position of having to decide what to do. For example, if the mortgagee proceeds by way of foreclosure and if the mortgagor finds that he or she will be able to bring the mortgage into good standing in the relatively near future, the mortgagor may file a notice D.O.R. (Desiring Opportunity to Redeem).

By filing a notice D.O.R., the mortgagor is automatically given the period of six months in which time the mortgage may be brought into good standing (which includes the payment of arrears of principal and interest and the costs of the mortgagee).

Alternatively, if the mortgagor wishes to have the property sold (in the hope that some of the proceeds will ultimately be paid to him or her) he or she may file a notice D.O.S. (Desiring Opportunity for Sale).

The effect of notice D.O.S. is to convert the foreclosure proceeding into a judicial sale of the premises. The right to file a notice D.O.R. or a notice D.O.S. is also available to a subsequent encumbrancer of the property.

If the mortgagor receives a notice of intention to sell under the power of private sale, he or she is then notified that a sale cannot be completed until a certain time (usually 35 days) has elapsed and at any time within this period the property may be redeemeed.

In addition, if the property is rented, the mortgagee may serve a notice of attornment on the tenant(s) which serves to direct that all subsequent rent payments be sent to the mortgagee instead of the mortgagor.

A mortgagor who is in default of mortgage obligations will usually be required to pay all of the costs and expenses which the mortgagee spends in order to protect the property and sue the mortgagor. For example, some of these expenses that may be incurred are taxes, insurance premiums, utility charges and repairs. In addition, the mortgagor is usually responsible for the payment of the legal costs of the mortgagee.

Further, these costs are usually payable on a "solicitor and client" basis. Solicitor and client costs are based on a higher scale than the scale of costs normally payable by an unsuccessful party in a litigation proceeding.

4. Fire insurance and mortgage default

The importance of adequate and proper fire insurance coverage on a home has been stressed throughout this book and this is especially important in the situation where a mortgagor is in default under the mortgage. Three aspects of the fire insurance coverage must be considered by the mortgagee when the mortgagor becomes in default:

(a) The premium for the fire insurance policy should be paid by the mortgagee, if it has not been paid by the mortgagor.

(b) Fire insurance coverage may be difficult to obtain by a mortgagee when the mortgagee has no control of the possession and use of the property.

(c) If the default of the mortgagor is accompanied by abandonment of the premises, the insurance company must be notified of the vacancy of the property.

It must be stressed that the above does not consider in detail all the aspects of the default situation. However, it can be seen that the mortgagor, the mortgagee and all other persons with an interest in the property have various rights. In order to protect these rights, it is vitally important for all parties concerned to seek legal assistance at the earliest possible date.

c. REFINANCING YOUR MORTGAGE

It often happens that a home owner needs to borrow a large amount of money and the only available source of borrowing money is the giving of a mortgage on his or her home. This situation may arise when a mortgage matures; when unexpected medical bills must be paid; when substantial repairs to the home are required; when the home owner becomes unemployed, or for many other reasons.

Most money lenders require a borrower to provide a form of security for the loan and one of the most acceptable forms of security to money lenders is a mortgage on residential real estate.

The media is full of advertisements asking us to cash in on our equity in our homes. If you have made the basic decision (after careful consideration) to mortgage your home, the following alternatives are open:

(a) Adding a subsequent mortgage to the existing mortgage or mortgages

(b) Replacing one or more of the existing mortgages with a new mortgage with a greater principal amount than the existing mortgage or mortgages being discharged

You must be concerned with the total amount of the carrying charges required under all of the mortgages. If this total amount exceeds your capacity, the second alternative should be considered. This will usually result in a lowering of the carrying charges. That may not necessarily be the better deal, however, because you may have to give up a relatively low rate of interest or pay a substantial amount of bonus in order to obtain a discharge of the existing mortgage. These factors should be carefully weighed before a decision is reached.

Because of the complexities involved, it is strongly suggested that if you are seeking money by way of mortgage financing, you should get the advice of a legal adviser.

The three most common ways of finding mortgage financing are as follows.

1. Inquiries through your lawyer

In many instances your lawyer may know another client who is interested in making a loan. The two clients can get together and arrange a deal between themselves. Many lawyers do not wish to do this type of work because by introducing one client to another, he or she will run the risk of being viewed with some disfavor by either or both of these clients at some later date if a dispute arises. In addition, a lawyer will have a "conflict of interest" problem by acting for both parties. Despite these problems, lawyers can and often do provide valuable contacts for persons seeking financing.

2. Personal loan

A home owner can seek a personal loan from a bank and, by way of collateral security, offer a mortgage on his or her home. A bank or lending institution under the Loan and Trusts Act is not allowed to place actual mortgage loans unless the mortgage is a first mortgage or unless the mortgage is given as collateral security to other security. This opens the door for the bank to use the mortgage for collateral security which they do as often as they can.

For example, if you require a loan of $3 000, you may borrow this from the bank giving the bank a promissory note as the principal security, an assignment of insurance policies and an additional mortgage on your residence as further collateral on the loan. However, for loans of this nature, banks will often want collateral security that can quickly be converted into cash (such as stocks or bonds or life insurance with a large cash surrender value) and, as previously mentioned, a mortgage may take several months to convert into cash. Therefore, in many situations, the bank may not wish to receive a mortgage as collateral security.

3. Contacting a mortgage broker

A mortgage broker is a person who buys or sells mortgages or who introduces a money lender and a money borrower, charging either one of them a fee for these services.

A mortgage broker deals in mortgages in the same way as a merchant deals in shoes, clothing, automobiles or any other product. He or she usually purchases a mortgage for less than the amount owing under the mortgage and will then attempt to resell this mortgage at a greater amount. For example, in a situation where you require the loan of $3 000, a mortgage broker may offer to loan you $3 000 on the security of a mortgage for $4 000, the remaining $1 000 being a bonus to the mortgage broker. The mortgage broker will then attempt to sell the mortgage to a third party for a price between $3 000 and $4 000, thus making a profit on the transaction.

The modern mortgage broker is able to stay in business because institutional lenders are governed by certain restrictive requirements in the making of mortgage loans. Common restrictions are that the mortgage be a first mortgage, that the income of the male spouse meet a certain minimum requirement, or that the amount loaned represents a maximum proportion of the value of the home.

Quite often, a mortgage broker will be able to place a mortgage that could not be placed with an institutional lender because the broker usually has access to money lenders who are willing to lend money at greater risks than a mortgage institution is able to take.

When you have found someone who is willing to lend the money, you must have an agreement between you. Once the lender is located, the parties enter into an "agreement to mortgage" (see Sample #17).

In addition to the agreement for mortgage, the Mortgage Brokers Act provides that a statement of mortgage must be signed and given to the borrower at least 24 hours before he or she is asked to sign any mortgage documents (see Sample #18). You will note that the statement of mortgage gives you a great deal of information about the transaction, some of which you may not have thought to ask.

The mortgage transaction will proceed in a manner very similar to the purchase and sale of a home, except, of course, that there will be no change of possession of the property and that the document given at the completion of the transaction is a mortgage, rather than a deed. In the course of the mortgage transaction, the mortgagee will do many of the things that a purchaser would do and the mortgagor does many of the things that the vendor must do.

The reason that a mortgage transaction approximates a purchase and sale transaction is that the mortgagee and his or her lawyer must be satisfied, in the same way as a purchaser would be, that the property is as described to the mortgagee so that, if the mortgagor defaults under the mortgage, the mortgagee will be able to obtain the property by a legal process and, subsequently, become the vendor of the property for the purposes of reselling the home to a third party.

Thus, the mortgagee, like a purchaser, must regard the property with a view that some day it might be necessary to sell it. It is common in the current mortgage market for the borrower to be required to pay the legal costs of the mortgagee's lawyer. These costs are usually the tariff amount for fees and disbursements in the amount that was spent by this lawyer. Of course, the borrower must also pay his or her own lawyer's charges.

d. SELLING THE MORTGAGE BACK

Often a vendor will accept a mortgage back as part payment for the sale of his or her home only to find that he or she requires the money rather than the mortgage. In this situation, the vendor will want to "cash out" the mortgage now instead of waiting for the term of the mortgage to expire.

In short, the vendor wants to exchange the mortgage back for money. The two most common ways of doing this are as follows:

(a) Borrowing money and assigning the mortgage to the lender of the money as security for the loan

(b) Selling the mortgage

The sale of a mortgage is a transaction that is usually entered into following an agreement (like an agreement of purchase and sale) and is conducted in a manner similar to the sale of a home. There is a date of closing and change of title (the title on the mortgage being changed rather than the ownership of the property).

SAMPLE #17
AGREEMENT TO MORTGAGE

Dye & Durham Limited — Law and Commercial Stationers
76 Richmond Street E., Toronto

FORM NO. 449

I, the undersigned, as purchaser, hereby agree with __VIOLET VENDOR__ as Vendor,

through __CONSCIENTIOUS REAL ESTATE LIMITED__ as Agent,

to purchase a __second__ Mortgage upon the property known as __1234 ANY STREET, TORONTO__

for the price of $ __6,200.00__ and I enclose herein $ __10.00__ cheque to the said agent on this date as a deposit, and I COVENANT AND AGREE to pay the remainder of the said price in cash or by certified cheque on the date of closing hereinafter mentioned.

This mortgage is subject to a prior mortgage for about __$24,851.17__

IT IS UNDERSTOOD AND AGREED by and between the parties that this sale is governed by the conditions contained below and the Purchaser acknowledges that he has read the said conditions and agrees that they shall govern this transaction.

This sale shall be completed on or before __July 18th, 1985__ and in the event that the purchaser fails to complete the transaction the deposit shall be forfeited as liquidated damages and not as a penalty.

Time shall be of the essence of this agreement.

CONDITIONS

1. The title to be good and free from encumbrances save as aforesaid.

2. The purchaser to be allowed seven days from the date hereof to investigate the title at his own expense, and if within that time he shall furnish the vendor in writing with any valid objection to the title which the vendor shall be unable or unwilling to remove, and which the purchaser will not waive, this agreement shall be null and void, and the deposit money returned to the purchaser without interest.

3. The vendor shall supply an assignment of mortgage duly executed, and a notice to the mortgagor, together with an acknowledgement or a declaration by the mortgagee verifying the principal outstanding upon the said mortgage, but the vendor shall not be bound to produce any abstract of title, deeds, copies of deeds, or other evidence of title except such as are in his possession or under his control.

4. It is understood and agreed by the vendor, and the vendor hereby warrants, that the mortgage stands at the sum of about $ __6,200.00__ on account of principal, together with interest thereon at the rate of __8½__ % per annum, repayable $ __100.00__ quarter-yearly/monthly; plus/including interest and that the mortgage has about __six__ years to run, and is XXrenewable, and that such mortgage is not in default. In the event that the said mortgage does not comply with these terms, subject to paragraph 6 below, then this contract is to be null and void and the purchaser is to have his deposit returned, without interest. The mortgage does contain a prepayment privilege.

5. The purchaser is to pay his own cost of investigating the title and for the registration of his documents.

6. The amount of the mortgage is approximate, and any difference in the amount shall be adjusted at the time of closing, upon a pro rata basis, provided that the difference shall not exceed 5% of the amount stated to be correct.

7. Accrued interest upon the mortgage shall be adjusted as of date of closing.

8. This offer upon acceptance shall with such acceptance constitute a binding contract of purchase and sale.

9. It is agreed that there is no representation, warranty, collateral agreement or condition affecting this agreement, the mortgage, or the real property or supported hereby other than as expressed herein in writing.

10. The purchaser acknowledges that he is relying upon his own inspection only as to the nature or condition of the property.

11. This offer to purchase shall be irrevocable by the Purchaser until 11.59 p.m. the __4th__ day of __July__, 1985 after which time, if not accepted, this offer to be null and void and deposit money to be returned to the purchaser without interest.

DATED at __Toronto__ this __4th__ day of __July__ 198-

(signed) _Arthur Agent_   _Marilyn Mortgagee_

Witness   Purchaser

ACCEPTANCE OF OFFER

I HEREBY accept the above offer and covenant and agree to carry out the covenants and conditions thereto, and I hereby agree to pay the said agent a commission of $ __200.00__ on the date above fixed for completion, in consideration of his services in procuring the above offer and I hereby authorize him to retain the said commission or any part thereof out of any deposit paid to him by the purchaser, on account of the purchased price, and I irrevocably instruct and authorize the purchaser or his solicitor to pay any unpaid balance of the commission from closing funds, to him on date above fixed for completion.

DATED at __Toronto__ this __4th__ day of __July__ 198-

(signed) _Arthur Agent_   (signed) _Violet Vendor_

Witness   Vendor

196

STATEMENT OF MORTGAGE

STATEMENT OF MORTGAGE

*This form must be completed in duplicate in accordance with the Regulations
under The Mortgage Brokers Act, 1968-69, and a signed copy given to the borrower at least 24 hours before he is asked to sign any mortgage documents.*

Property Mortgaged (address and description of buildings) 1234 Any Street,
Toronto, being the whole of Lot 62, according to Plan 10572, Toronto

1. Principal amount of the ___regular___ ; ___second___
   (REGULAR OR COLLATERAL)   (1ST, 2ND, 3RD)

   Mortgage to be repaid by the Borrower $ 6,200.00

2. Deduct Bonus, Charges, Fees, etc. (This amount must equal total items under Section 8) $ Nil

3. Amount of money to be paid to the Borrower or to be disbursed on his direction is $ 6,200.00

4. THE MAXIMUM ANNUAL EFFECTIVE RATE OF INTEREST ON THIS MORTGAGE IS $10\frac{1}{2}$ %
   (This rate will be higher than the rate shown below in item 5, whenever there is a bonus charged).

5. The Principal amount of the Mortgage (item 1) of $ 6,200.00 will bear interest at $8\frac{1}{2}$ % per year

   and will be repayable in ___quarterly___ instalments of $ 100.00 plus _____ interest.
   (MONTHLY OR QUARTERLY)   (PLUS OR INCLUDING)

6. The Mortgage will become due and payable in 6 years at which time the Borrower, if all
   payments are made on the due date will owe $ 3,800.00

7. The Mortgage is not renewable on the same terms as item 5 above and does not contain any
   privileges or penalties except as follows: 1) Open in whole or in part at any time or
                                               times;
   2) Renewable for a further 4 years with interest at $10\frac{1}{2}$%;
   3) Privilege allowing Mortgagors to renew or replace prior first Mortgage.

8. The BONUS, Charges, Fees, etc., to be deducted from the Principal amount of the Mortgage under item 2 above,
   are made up as follows:
   BONUS on Mortgage $ NIL
   Brokerage Fees or Commissions $ NIL
   Inspection and Appraisal Fees $ NIL
   Lawyer's Fees and Estimated Disbursements of not more than $ NIL
   Other Charges $ NIL $ NIL
   TOTAL as shown in item 2 above $ NIL

This Mortgage shall be arranged on or before the   30th day of June   19 8-

I, WE, PETER PURCHASER & PAULA PURCHASER, of 1234 ANY STREET, TORONTO
         NAME   ADDRESS

the Borrower/under this proposed Mortgage, have read and fully understand the above Statement furnished us by
VIOLET VENDOR,
                              NAME AND ADDRESS OF BROKER

I/We have not yet signed any Mortgage Papers or Blank Documents on this mortgage and now sign this Statement in
we duplicate, which has been fully completed this 28th day of June   19 8- , and
I/we hereby acknowledge receipt of a fully completed signed copy.

                                        (signed) *Peter Purchaser*
                                        (signed) *Paula Purchaser*
                                                 Signature of Borrower

I VIOLET VENDOR _____ have fully completed the above Statement
          NAME OF BROKER

in duplicate and have furnished one signed copy to the Borrower on the above date.

                                        (signed) *Violet Vendor*
                                                 Signature of Broker

197

On the closing of a transaction for sale of a mortgage, the document evidencing the transfer of title is a "transfer of charge" or an "assignment of mortgage," depending on where the land is registered and this document approximates a deed or transfer in a transaction where real estate is sold.

Of course, there is no change of possession in the property and, in fact, the owner of the property is only peripherally involved in the transaction.

If the terms of the mortgage are not consistent with those available on the current market or, if it is necessary to sell the mortgage through a mortgage broker, it will probably be necessary to sell the mortgage at an amount less than face value, commonly called at a "discount."

For example, if a vendor has taken back a mortgage for $7 000 with interest at 9%, based on a 25-year amortization and a 5-year term, and if the purchaser of this mortgage wishes to earn 10½% on his or her money, the purchaser will offer to purchase the mortgage at a discount of approximately $400. The amount of a discount in any particular transaction, of course, is subject to agreement between the vendor and purchaser of the mortgage.

e. CONDITIONAL SALES CONTRACTS

When a home owner is required to replace or purchase a major article for use in the home, such as a new furnace, a conditional sales contract may be drawn up between the seller of the article and the home owner.

The conditional sales contract will require the payment of certain instalments by the home owner over a period of time and the seller may wish to register a notice of the conditional sales contract on the title to the property in order to provide some security for the payment.

The seller of the article may register such a notice of conditional sales contract without the home owner having any knowledge of its registration. In this situation, the owner of the property will not be aware of the encumbrance created by the registration of the notice of conditional sales contract until the property is sold, which may be some time after the last payment was made to the vendor.

When a home owner purchases a major article, such as a furnace, and signs a conditional sales contract, it should be ascertained if the seller will be registering a notice of the conditional sales contract on the title to the property. If the answer is "Yes," the home owner should make sure that a release of the notice of conditional sales agreement is obtained when making the final payment under the contract.

f. CONSTRUCTING ADDITIONS TO THE HOME

Gone are the days when a home owner with a week's spare time can simply erect a garage or other structure.

When a home owner wishes to make an addition to his home, such as an extra room or swimming pool, there are potential problem areas that must be attended to before starting construction.

The first matter that the home owner should look into is the effect that the addition will have on his or her mortgage. Construction on real estate may technically be considered to be "waste," regardless of the fact that it may be beneficial to the property, and, under the law of mortgages, a mortgagor cannot commit waste. Thus, the home owner should ask the mortgagee for a consent or acknowledgment from the mortgagee that the proposed addition will not be considered to be waste.

The next matter to consider is the location of the proposed addition. As previously stated, if there is an easement over a section of the property, you cannot construct on this easement without facing substantial risks. Accordingly, you must make sure that the proposed addition or alteration will not in any way deleteriously affect the rights of an owner of an easement.

The next matter to be considered is the zoning by-law. The zoning by-law must be consulted in order to make sure that the proposed alteration or addition will be allowed.

This is done by consulting the "use" portion of the zoning by-law.

Secondly, the zoning by-law usually contains setback requirements. These setback requirements are usually minimum distances from the various lot lines in which a home owner is prohibited from erecting a form of construction.

If the proposed addition or alteration is in contravention of the zoning by-law, to a minor extent, it is possible to make an application to the committee of adjustment in the municipality in which the property is located in order to obtain the consent to a "minor variance."

If the committee of adjustment approves the proposed addition or alteration, the home owner may proceed to construct the addition or alteration, notwithstanding that it is in contravention of the zoning by-law. If there is a problem here, the advice and assistance of a legal adviser will be required.

You must also obtain a building permit from the building department of the municipality in which the property is located. It will be necessary to have detailed plans of the proposed alteration or addition which requires the drawing or purchase of detailed plans. Finally, if you are hiring a contractor, you should also be aware of the problems of construction liens.

g. CONSTRUCTION LIENS

Construction liens are discussed in chapter 3. The purpose here is to point out that you may be living in a home and have a construction lien registered against the title and not realize it until the time the home is sold.

In other words, if you require work or services to be performed on the home, such as adding a bedroom, repairing the plumbing, installing a swimming pool, or paving a driveway, a construction lien right may be registered against the land without you being aware of its existence.

The Construction Lien Act provides that an owner of real estate is required to hold back from the payments due to the contractor. This amount of holdback is to be retained by the owner of land and held in trust as security for the subcontractors of the contractor or the employees of the subcontractor or contractor in order to make sure that these people have been paid. If they have, no lien will be registered.

However, if these people have not been paid and if they have registered a lien, the owner of the land may wish to pay the holdback into court in order to have the lien removed from the title to the property.

Thus, to be entirely safe in paying the holdback, you should search the title to your property after the work has been completed. Also, if you are considering substantial construction or repair to the actual house, you should become aware of the provisions of the Construction Lien Act. In order to properly protect yourself against problems under this act, get advice from your lawyer before entering into any contract for construction or repair of the home.

h. INVESTING IN MORTGAGES

Mortgages are a popular investment for many people. The rate of return can vary from market interest rates for first mortgages to which that rate or even more for second or third mortgages. There is usually a direct correlation between the rate of return and the risk factor; the higher the return, the higher the risk.

Most investing is done through mortgage brokers who find the mortgagor, make the mortgage agreement (and perhaps close the deal), and then sell it. When dealing with a mortgage broker, whether you are arranging a loan or investing, you should be as selective and careful as when dealing with a used car salesperson.

Generally speaking, the mortgage broker, or the person selling the mortgage, will be responsible for preparing all legal documentation to assign the mortgage to the investor and will bear the costs of doing so.

When investing in a mortgage, you should check or verify the following basic essentials before the purchase money is paid over:

(a) The legal description in the mortgage and the civic address of the property which is mortgaged should correspond and should represent the same property.

(b) There should be insurance on the property for an amount equal, at least, to the outstanding amounts of all the mortgages with loss payable to the assignee of the mortgage as that interest may appear.

(c) The balance owing on the mortgage and the monthly payments should be confirmed by the person making the payments.

(d) Not only should the mortgage be assigned and the assignment registered, but a notice of the assignment should also be completed and given to the person making the payments.

(e) The investor should be satisfied that there is some equity in the property. The more equity there is, the more protection. The less equity there is, the higher the interest rate. The investor must decide whether it is better to receive a higher interest rate and bear a higher risk or receive a lower interest rate and bear a lower risk. If there is no equity in the property, there is very little incentive to the mortgagor to make the payments.

(f) The investment money should not be paid to the mortgage broker but only to the broker's solicitor against a written undertaking not to release the money until the required mortgage interest is obtained. Money can also be paid to the investor's own lawyer, who will then look after and protect the investor's interests. The investor will, unless it has been negotiated otherwise, be responsible for that lawyer's fees.

(g) As mentioned, generally speaking, it is the mortgage broker who pays for the cost of assigning the mortgage to the investor. In any event, the investor should clearly ascertain, before purchasing or agreeing to purchase a mortgage, who will be paying the lawyer.

(h) Mortgage brokerage is governed by the Mortgage Brokers Act. This act provides that, where the borrower is charged with a brokerage fee or a commission, the borrower is required to be presented with a disclosure statement before signing the mortgage. This disclosure statement gives full disclosure to the borrower of the true cost of the mortgage. It is called a "statement of mortgage" and is illustrated in Sample #18. This form must be presented to and signed by the borrower at least 24 hours before the borrower is asked to sign any mortgage documents.

APPENDIX

ONTARIO NEW HOME WARRANTY PROGRAM OFFICES

Hamilton (serving Hamilton and Niagara)
883 Upper Wentworth Street
Suite 204
Hamilton L9A 4Y6
(416) 575-7377

Kitchener (serving South-Western Ontario)
385 Frederick Street
(Mall), Main Floor
Kitchener N2H 2P2
(519) 744-0861 / (519) 744-0861

Ottawa (serving Eastern Ontario)
190 Colonnade Road
Centre Block, 2nd Floor
Nepean K2E 7J5
(613) 727-0346

Sudbury (serving Northern Ontario)
Unit C
Cedar Point Shopping Plaza
1984 Regent Street S.
Sudbury P3E 5S1
(705) 522-2522

Thunder Bay (serving North Western Ontario)
91 Cumberland Street S.
Suite 215
Thunder Bay P7B 6A7
(807) 345-2026

Toronto (serving Central Ontario)
600 Eglinton Avenue E.
Toronto M4P 1P3
(416) 488-6000

CANADIAN
ORDER FORM
SELF-COUNSEL SERIES

SELF-COUNSEL SERIES

05/87

NATIONAL TITLES:

Abbreviations & Acronyms	5.95
Aids to Independence	11.95
Asking Questions	7.95
Assertiveness for Managers	8.95
Basic Accounting	5.95
Be a Better Manager	8.95
Best Ways to Make Money	5.95
Better Book for Getting Hired	9.95
Between the Sexes	8.95
Business Guide to Effective Speaking	6.95
Business Guide to Telephone Systems	7.95
Business Writing Workbook	9.95
Buying (and Selling) a Small Business	6.95
Civil Rights	8.95
Collection Techniques for the Small Business	4.95
Complete Guide to Home Contracting	19.95
Conquering Compulsive Eating	5.95
Credit, Debt, and Bankruptcy	7.95
Criminal Procedure in Canada	14.95
Design Your Own Logo	9.95
Drinking and Driving	4.50
Editing Your Newsletter	14.95
Entrepreneur's Self-Assessment Guide	9.95
Family Ties That Bind	7.95
Federal Incorporation and Business Guide	14.95
Financial Control for the Small Business	6.95
Financial Freedom on $5 a Day	7.95
For Sale By Owner	6.95
Forming and Managing a Non-Profit Organization in Canada	12.95
Franchising in Canada	6.50
Fundraising	5.50
Getting Elected	8.95
Getting Sales	14.95
Getting Started	10.95
How to Advertise	7.95
How You Too Can Make a Million . . . in the Mail Order Business	9.95
Immigrating to Canada	14.95
Immigrating to U.S.A.	14.95
Insuring Business Risks	3.50
Keyboarding for Kids	7.95
Landlording in Canada	12.95
Learn to Type Fast	9.95
Managing Your Office Records & Files	14.95
Managing Stress	7.95
Marketing Your Service	12.95
Media Law Handbook	6.50
Medical Law Handbook	6.95
Mike Grenby's Tax Tips	6.95
Mortgages & Foreclosure	7.95
Musician's Handbook	7.95
A Nanny For Your Child	7.95
Newcomer's Guide to the U.S.A.	12.95
Parent's Guide to Day Care	5.95
Patent Your Own Invention	21.95
Photography & The Law	7.95
Practical Guide to Financial Management	6.95
Radio Documentary Handbook	8.95
Ready-to-Use Business Forms	9.95
Retirement Guide for Canadians	9.95
Small Business Guide to Employee Selection	6.95
Start and Run a Profitable Beauty Salon	14.95
Start and Run a Profitable Consulting Business	12.95
Start and Run a Profitable Craft Business	10.95
Start and Run a Profitable Home Typing Business	9.95
Start and Run a Profitable Restaurant	10.95
Start and Run a Profitable Retail Business	11.95
Start and Run a Profitable Video Store	10.95
Starting a Successful Business in Canada	12.95
Step-Parent Adoptions	12.95
Taking Care	7.95
Tax Law Handbook	12.95
Tax Shelters	7.95
Trusts and Trust Companies	3.95
Upper Left-Hand Corner	10.95
Using the Access to Information Act	5.95
Word Processing	8.95
Working Couples	5.50
Write Right!	5.50

PROVINCIAL TITLES:

Divorce Guide
□ B.C. 9.95 □ Alberta 9.95 □ Ontario 12.95
□ Manitoba 11.95 □ Saskatchewan

Employer/Employee Rights
□ B.C. 6.95 □ Alberta 6.95 □ Ontario 6.95

Fight That Ticket
□ B.C. 5.95

Incorporation Guide
□ B.C. 14.95 □ Alberta 14.95 □ Ontario 14.95
□ Manitoba/Saskatchewan 12.95

Landlord/Tenant Rights
□ B.C. 7.95 □ Alberta 6.95 □ Ontario 7.95

Marriage & Family Law
□ B.C. 7.95 □ Alberta 8.95 □ Ontario 7.95

Probate Guide
□ B.C. 12.95 □ Alberta 9.95 □ Ontario 11.95

Real Estate Guide
□ B.C. 7.95 □ Alberta 7.95 □ Ontario

Small Claims Court Guide
□ B.C. 7.95 □ Alberta 7.50 □ Ontario 7.50

Wills
□ B.C. 6.50 □ Alberta 5.95 □ Ontario 5.95

Wills/Probate Procedure
□ Manitoba/Saskatchewan 5.95

PACKAGED FORMS:

Divorce Forms
□ B.C. 9.95 □ Alberta 10.95 □ Ontario 14.95
□ Manitoba 10.95 □ Saskatchewan 12.95

Incorporation
□ B.C. 12.95 □ Alberta 14.95 □ Ontario 14.95
□ Manitoba 14.95 □ Saskatchewan 14.95 □ Federal 7.95

Minute Books 17.95

Probate
□ B.C. Administration 14.95 □ B.C. Probate 14.95 □ Alberta 14.95
□ Ontario 15.50

□ Rental Form Kit (B.C., Alberta, Ontario, Saskatchewan)   5.95

□ Have You Made Your Will?   5.95

□ If You Love Me Put It In Writing   Contract Kit   14.95

□ If You Leave Me Put It In Writing   B.C. Separation Agreement Kit   14.95

NOTE: All prices are subject to change without notice.

Books are available in book and department stores, or use the order form below.

Please enclose cheque or money order (plus sales tax where applicable) or give us your MasterCard or Visa number (please include validation and expiry date).

(PLEASE PRINT)

Name _____

Address _____

City _____ Province _____ Postal Code _____

□ Visa/□ MasterCard Number _____

Validation Date _____ Expiry Date _____

If order is under $20.00, add $1.00 for postage and handling.

Please send orders to:

INTERNATIONAL SELF-COUNSEL PRESS LTD.   □ Check here for free catalogue.
1481 Charlotte Road
North Vancouver, British Columbia
V7J 1H1